LEICESTER CITY
Miscellany

LEICESTER CITY
Miscellany

Foxes Trivia,
History, Facts & Stats

MATT BOZEAT

LEICESTER CITY
Miscellany

All statistics, facts and figures are correct as of 1st August 2009

© Matt Bozeat

Matt Bozeat has asserted his rights in accordance with the Copyright, Designs and Patents Act 1988 to be identified as the author of this work.

Published By:
Pitch Publishing (Brighton) Ltd
A2 Yeoman Gate
Yeoman Way
Durrington
BN13 3QZ

Email: info@pitchpublishing.co.uk
Web: www.pitchpublishing.co.uk

First published 2009

A catalogue record for this book is available from the British Library.

10-digit ISBN: 1-9054114-1-3
13-digit ISBN: 978-1-9054114-1-2

Printed and bound in Malta by Gutenberg Press

FOREWORD BY STEVE WALSH

I was honoured to be asked by Matt to write a few words introducing this book and in the same breath daunted by trying to squeeze my thoughts about this great club into a concise space.

What can you say about Leicester City Football Club that hasn't already been said? Every time I donned the famous blue shirt I gave my all for the club I love. The fans, the history and thousands of other reasons, personal to me, but I'm sure you share them, are why I call Leicester my home and why I still support the club today.

We have often been branded as a yo-yo club, leaping between divisions whilst struggling to hold on to our best players. But, we've had some really special days and there are bound to be many more. Often we've been underdogs and created a siege mentality which has seen us through. You were all as much of a part of that as I was. Cut us all in half and we'd bleed blue blood.

I hope you enjoy this book whilst reminiscing through some great stories. All the best.

Steve Walsh,
Leicester City, 1986–2000

INTRODUCTION

So what exactly is a Miscellany?

According to my bosses, it's a collection of stories put together in no particular order and this one is all about my favourite football team.

I hope it makes you smile.

Matt Bozeat, 2009

SPIDER IS THE MAN!

There are those – members of his family mainly – who believe that Zeljko 'Spider' Kalac had a massive role in helping Leicester City into the Premier League without touching the ball.

Kalac was a big signing in every sense – he cost £760,000 from Sydney United and stood 6ft 7ins tall – and was an even bigger flop.

Boss Mark McGhee confidently predicted the Aussie international would go on to join Gordon Banks, Peter Shilton and Mark Wallington as a Leicester goalkeeping legend. He was wrong. Quite spectacularly wrong.

Kalac gifted West Bromwich Albion two goals on his debut at the Hawthorns in November, 1995 and was responsible for all Bolton Wanderers' goals in a 3-2 League Cup defeat three days later. He wasn't seen again until the dying seconds of the play-off final against Crystal Palace at Wembley.

The scores were locked at 1-1 when Leicester boss Martin O'Neill brought on Kalac for Kevin Poole with the game ticking towards a penalty shoot-out and City preparing to take a free kick.

Many City fans groaned, but there's a theory that his introduction distracted Palace and Steve Claridge popped up to shin home after Garry Parker's free kick wasn't cleared.

The final whistle went seconds later and City were promoted. Kalac hadn't touched the ball and that's probably just as well really.

Kalac never played for Leicester again, but McGhee kept faith in him and lined up a transfer for 'Spider' after taking over at Wolverhampton Wanderers following his controversial decision to walk away from Filbert Street. Problems gaining a work permit meant the deal never went through and Foxes fans were left rubbing their eyes in disbelief several seasons later when Kalac went on to join AC Milan and was on the bench for the Italians in a Champions League clash against Manchester United.

Leicester has a proud tradition of producing top-class goalkeepers. Horace Bailey was the club's first shot-stopper to play for England. He conceded just three goals in his five appearances for his country in 1908 – and the following year shipped 12 in one match while playing in an East Midlands derby! Bailey was the overworked goalkeeper when Nottingham Forest inflicted Leicester's record defeat by a 12-0 scoreline on April 21st, 1909 in a Division One fixture. Fosse went on to finish bottom of the table.

THE FUTURE'S BRIGHT WITHOUT GARY

The Football League's fixture computer was at its most mischievous in the summer of 1985.

A few weeks after leaving Leicester City for Everton in an £800,000 transfer, Gary Lineker discovered he would be heading back to Filbert Street to make his debut for the Toffeemen.

Although expected, Lineker's decision to leave Leicester still hurt supporters he had stood alongside as a boy.

He remembers crying all the way home from Wembley in 1969 after the FA Cup Final defeat against Manchester City and when asked in a football magazine to name his 'favourite other team', Lineker's reply was Leicester reserves!

But after 103 goals in 216 games for City, the prospect of playing for the Division One champions proved to be greater than that of another season spent battling in mid table and afternoons off playing a few frames of snooker with Willie Thorne.

So, Lineker went to Merseyside and then came back to face the club and supporters he had left behind. His place in Leicester's starting line-up went to Mark Bright and he had hardly set Filbert Street alight in his first season after joining from Port Vale. Although he failed to find the target, Bright did score 28 goals in 27 games for the reserves and was the obvious choice to replace Lineker in City's forward line when the 1985-86 season kicked off.

At the other end of the pitch, City boss Gordon Milne handed a debut to Russell Osman at the heart of the defence following his £240,000 move from Ipswich Town and while he was one of the heroes of Leicester's stunning 3-1 win, the following day's newspaper headlines were all about Bright. Bobby Smith cancelled out Everton's early opener and then Bright smacked a couple of belters past Welsh international Neville Southall to wrap up a sensational 3-1 win.

Julie Welch wrote in *The Observer*: "As the champions stumbled to their first pratfall of the season, the locals showed their sympathy for Lineker's poor showing with a rousing chorus of: 'What a waste of money.'"

Bright failed to build on that stunning performance, however. He netted only four more times for City, the fans barracked him and he went on to have success at Crystal Palace where he finished top scorer in Division Two, played in the top flight and the 1990 FA Cup Final and formed a partnership with Ian Wright.

After hanging up their boots, Lineker and Bright ended up on the same side as football pundits for the BBC.

A TALE OF TWO BROTHERS

For the benefit of the press, Allan Clarke arrived at Leicester City in a wheelbarrow – he was going to score a barrow load of goals – and two decades later, brother Wayne was similarly wheeled out to face the photographers at Filbert Street.

The difference is, Wayne probably left in a wheelbarrow as well.

He couldn't match his big brother's achievements. In June, 1968, City smashed the British transfer record when boss Matt Gillies got the backing of the club's board to spend £150,000 on Fulham striker Allan Clarke.

Leicester paid the Cottagers £110,000 and the fee was made up by Frank Large making the move in the opposite direction to London. A slender and stylish striker, Clarke got his City career off to the perfect start with

LEICESTER'S FAVOURITE SPORTING SON — AND NUMBER ONE CRISP THIEF — GARY LINEKER.

a debut goal in the 1-1 draw at Queens Park Rangers on the opening day of the season. Eleven days later, he looked worth every penny of Leicester's investment when a stunning hat-trick beat Manchester City at Filbert Street.

City ended up in a relegation battle, however, and Clarke's languid displays attracted criticism. He saved his best displays for the big occasion – and they don't get much bigger than the FA Cup semi-final. City faced holders West Bromwich Albion in the last four at Hillsborough and Clarke bagged the only goal with less than three minutes left to send City through to their third FA Cup Final in the 1960s. Again, Clarke was City's top performer on the big day.

Leicester were beaten 1-0 by Neil Young's strike, but it was 'Sniffer' who took the man-of-the-match award. After the final defeat, City had five games left to preserve their top-flight status and although Clarke got the only goal against Tottenham Hotspur three days after the defeat at Wembley, Leicester were relegated.

Clarke wasn't keen on playing in Division Two and his 16 goals in 46 appearances for City was enough to attract an offer from Leeds United that re-wrote the British transfer fee record for the second time in the space of 12 months. Clarke left for a fee of £165,000 and City made a £15,000 profit.

In the summer of 1989, Clarke's brother Wayne headed to Filbert Street from Everton as part of the deal that took Mike Newell to Merseyside.

Like his brother 21 years earlier, Clarke marked his Leicester debut with a goal in a 1-1 draw at Hull City, but netted only once more and left for Manchester City just seven months after arriving at City.

WHAT A GOAL!

Joey Gudjonsson looked up and saw that Hull City goalkeeper Boaz Myhill had wandered off his goal line. He then put down his binoculars, took aim and launched a shot from the halfway line that sailed over Myhill's head, into the net and into this book on the page that chronicles the most spectacular goals scored by Leicester City players.

The Icelandic international went on to add the winner in City's 3-2 victory in the Championship fixture at the Walkers Stadium in March, 2006.

As you will read elsewhere – if you get that far – Peter Shilton got on the score-sheet when playing in goal at Southampton in October, 1967 and another who found the target from long range was Dennis Rofe.

He belted home a free kick from just inside his own half in a 2-2 draw against Queens Park Rangers at Filbert Street in September, 1976. Rofe remembers this goal rather differently to everyone else who saw it. He reckons it was a tremendous bit of opportunism on his part. Everyone else says it was a fluke!

That word featured prominently in City's dressing room at the start of the 2003-2004 Premier League campaign and it was directed at French midfielder Lilian Nalis. He arrived at the Walkers Stadium in the summer of 2003 and his unstoppable volley sent City on their way to a 4-0 win over Leeds United in front of the Sky Sports cameras in September.

"Lilian doesn't speak much English," said City boss Micky Adams, "but he knows what the word fluke means now!"

The previous season, Muzzy Izzet left fans breathless with a stunning overhead kick that secured a 2-1 win for ten-man City at Grimsby Town and mention must be made of Alan Birchenall's howitzer against Leeds United at Filbert Street in October, 1973.

Later that season, Keith Weller danced through the Kenilworth Road mud and then smacked a left-foot shot into the top corner that put the seal on a 4-0 win at Luton Town in the fifth round of the FA Cup that is remembered as one of City's finest performances of their flamboyant 1970s pomp.

Julian Joachim's haul of 31 goals for Leicester include some spectacular strikes. As a teenage whizzkid, he bagged the BBC's Goal of the Month award for his solo goal in an FA Cup third round replay at

Barnsley in January, 1993. Better still was his blistering run and cheeky poke through the goalkeeper's legs in the play-off semi-final against Portsmouth later that season.

EUROPEAN ADVENTURES

If you see a Leicester City player at an airport, chances are he's off on his holidays. To date, the club have only made three appearances in European competition. In 1961, they qualified for the European Cup Winners' Cup by virtue of losing to double winners Tottenham Hotspur in the FA Cup Final.

After beating Irish team Glenavon 7-2 on aggregate in the first round, City bowed out to Atletico Madrid. Ken Keyworth netted for City in a 1-1 draw at Filbert Street and the second leg was lost 2-0 in Spain. Thirty-six years later, Atletico provided the opposition again on City's return to Europe after they had lifted the League Cup with victory over Middlesbrough in a replay at Hillsborough to qualify for the UEFA Cup.

Ian Marshall stunned the Spaniards by putting City ahead in the first leg in Madrid. Two late goals gave the home side victory and they were 2-0 winners at Filbert Street in the return after City were controversially denied penalties and had Garry Parker controversially sent off.

City's League Cup triumph in 2000 led to another short-lived European adventure. Martin O'Neill's team fell behind in the first minute to Yugoslav double winners Red Star Belgrade in the first leg at Filbert Street and Gerry Taggart popped up with the equaliser.

The second leg was played in Vienna because of political unrest in Serbia and Muzzy Izzet was City's marksman in a 3-1 defeat.

The club's first journey into Europe had actually come in the summer of 1913 – and had proved to be much more successful. After having Swedish international Karl Gustafsson on loan, Fosse were offered an all-expenses paid trip to Sweden by the country's FA and on June 16th, they set off on a 46-hour sea and rail journey to Gothenburg.

Incredibly, Fosse played their first game only two hours after arriving in Sweden – and were still able to record a 3-2 win over an Orgryte/ IFK Goteborg Select Team. They went on to win all five games on the whirlwind ten-day tour and that included two victories over a full Swedish international line-up. Prince Eugene was among the crowd for Fosse's second win by a 4-2 scoreline.

Fred Mortimer, Fosse's newly-signed striker, was on the score-sheet in all five games and ended up with 10 goals on the tour. Fosse's players were each presented with a commemorative silver cup and arrangements were made for another Swedish international, Helge Ekroth, to spend a loan spell at Filbert Street during the following season.

SEVEN MINUTES OF MAYHEM

The drama didn't end when the referee finally blew his whistle to end Leicester City's astonishing 3-3 draw with Arsenal at Filbert Street in August, 1997. Just ask Steve Walsh. Or rather, don't ask him.

The decision to allow seven minutes of added time gave Walsh enough time to power home a late leveller and the Gunners were so incensed that several players surrounded the officials to protest. Ian Wright even raced off the substitutes' bench to get his point across and Walsh, never one to back down, met him head on.

"The question I get asked the most," recalled the Leicester legend "is what I said to Wright when he came running onto the pitch. The thing is, I'd rather not say. I always tell people I can't remember."

Nobody who was there and didn't leave early will ever forget the late drama that led to the confrontation. City were 2-0 behind after 83 minutes and went on to snatch a point after Dennis Bergkamp's hat-trick had looked like winning it for the Gunners.

Along with his wholehearted commitment and crucial goals, Walsh is also remembered for his feuds and battles with Wolverhampton Wanderers striker Steve Bull which provided a compelling subplot to matches between the sides.

In fact, you suspect there were those who went to the games just to watch their duel. Walsh admitted his instructions were to "give him a kick early on to slow him down a bit" and he got a black eye for doing just that in November, 1989 during a Division Two clash at Filbert Street. Bull was given a red card for giving Walsh a shiner and the roles were reversed in August, 1992. This time it was Walsh running the taps ahead of schedule after an off-the-ball bust up.

In total, Walsh was sent off nine times while playing for City – a club record. He is also among the leading appearance makers for Leicester having played 449 games during 14 years at Filbert Street after joining from Wigan Athletic. He proved to be effective at both ends of the pitch and perhaps his finest moment came in the play-off final at Wembley in May, 1994. It looked like Walsh's season was over eight months earlier after a cruciate ligament injury he suffered at Middlesbrough. He battled back to fitness, though, and his goal double against Derby County sent Brian Little's team into the Premier League and secured the Foxes' first win at Wembley at the seventh attempt.

I WILL GET MY COAT

Peter Eccles wasn't the type to outstay his welcome. He is remembered for having one of the shortest international careers having played just 10 minutes for the Republic of Ireland – and he didn't hang around for long at Leicester City either.

David Pleat handed Eccles his debut at the heart of City's defence at Blackburn Rovers in March, 1989 – in the absence of Steve Walsh – and he was substituted at half time. City went on to draw at Ewood Park 0-0 and Eccles never played for City again.

The distinction of the shortest-ever Leicester City career is shared by Malcolm Clarke and Tommy Williamson. Both came on in the 89th minute of fixtures; Clarke came on in the dying moments of a home match against Leeds United in September, 1965 and Williamson earned a footnote in Filbert Street's history by replacing Muzzy Izzet in the final game at the ground against Tottenham Hotspur in May, 2002.

Compared to them, Kevin Ellison was a Leicester stalwart. His Foxes career lasted six minutes! At least the striker plucked from non-league Altrincham by boss Peter Taylor got to play at Old Trafford – and he can say that his introduction was the turning point. The scores were level when he came on in the 84th minute – and Manchester United ended up winning the game 2-0.

Luigi Glombard wore Leicester's colours for just ten minutes. He joined on loan from Cardiff City and came off the bench in the 2-0 win at Ipswich Town in February, 2007 before returning to Wales.

Sascha Lenhart's contribution to Leicester City winning their first piece of silverware for 33 years was just 49 minutes. The winger came on in the League Cup clash against Scarborough at Filbert Street in September, 1996. Lenhart never got another chance for Leicester and probably didn't even notice when Martin O'Neill's team went on to lift the trophy seven months later.

Kevin Reed came on as a second-half substitute in the clash with Wrexham in November, 1978 and he didn't do enough to get another chance from Leicester boss Jock Wallace.

Graham Brown was another not to complete 90 minutes. He came on for John Sjoberg in the second half of the 1-0 win over Aston Villa at Filbert Street in April, 1970.

James Campbell was a regular for City in fixtures during the Second World War, but his first-class career lasted less than 90 minutes as he suffered a head injury in an FA Cup clash at Chelsea in January, 1946.

MANAGERS ON THE MOVE

Above all else, football fans demand a bit of loyalty and that's why you probably won't see Brian Little or Mark McGhee doing their shopping at the Highcross. In the space of 12 months, both walked out of Filbert Street and it is doubtful either will ever be forgiven by Leicester City supporters. City were in disarray when Little arrived in the summer of 1991 having previously steered Darlington to back-to-back promotions. Leicester had escaped relegation to the third tier of English football for the first time in their history and Little set about rebuilding the club's fortunes. At the third attempt, he took City into the Premier League via the play-offs with victory over Derby County following defeats in the previous two finals at Wembley against Blackburn Rovers and Swindon Town.

Following promotion, City were immediately installed as favourites to be relegated and set about ensuring the gamblers weren't disappointed. They had to wait until their sixth game for a first victory – Julian Joachim on target twice in a memorable 3-1 win over Ossie Ardiles' Tottenham Hotspur at Filbert Street – and the rumours started that Little would be on his way back to Villa Park after Ron Atkinson was sacked by Villa.

Little actually cited personal reasons for his decision to resign as Leicester manager in November 1994 and whatever those personal reasons were, they didn't prevent him becoming Villa boss four days after leaving Filbert Street.

Cue outrage in Leicester and thankfully for Foxes fans, they got the chance to let Little know exactly what they thought of him later that month when Villa came to Filbert Street. He was booed, heckled and hissed at throughout the 1-1 draw.

McGhee left Reading to take on the job and although a 4-4 draw at Little's Villa when City clawed back a 4-1 deficit with only 13 minutes left raised hopes of an escape, Leicester were relegated. The Scot's team played some dazzling football at the start of the 1995-96 season as they set about earning promotion. Then history repeated itself.

Wolverhampton Wanderers sacked their manager; McGhee got itchy feet and was off. Cue more outrage in Leicester. City did get their revenge with a 3-2 win at Molineux in February that was Martin O'Neill's first win as Leicester manager. Thankfully, O'Neill hung around for a while.

More than a decade earlier, Jock Wallace's decision to leave Filbert Street for Motherwell in the summer of 1982 caused similar fury. A few months earlier, he had taken City to the FA Cup semi final.

WHAT MIGHT HAVE BEEN

Both grew up supporting Leicester City and idolising Frank Worthington. Gary Lineker made his boyhood dreams come true, Richard Hill was the one that got away.

As a teenager, Hill, raised in Hinckley, was on City's books, but he failed to make a first-team appearance and joined non-league Nuneaton Borough in 1983. A move to Northampton Town followed and Hill's haul of 33 goals from midfield in the 1986-87 season helped the Cobblers romp to the Division Four championship and earned a £240,000 move to Watford – in the days when £240,000 was a lot of money.

Hill was hit by injuries, however, and after a transfer to Oxford United, he went on to play for Leicestershire non-league side Shepshed Dynamo. He made an appearance at Filbert Street with Dynamo in the County Cup final in 1997-98 and was denied an early goal against Leicester by the woodwork before the Foxes ran out 6-1 winners.

Tony Thorpe is another who went on to be a prolific goal scorer in the lower leagues after being released by his home-town club. He had the satisfaction of netting for Luton Town in a 1-1 draw at Filbert Street in February, 1996, but another return to Leicester with Bristol City for an FA Cup fifth round tie in February, 2001 ended in a 3-0 defeat.

Carl Heggs also suffered FA Cup heartbreak at Filbert Street. Although never on City's books, Heggs made no secret of his affection for his home-town club and came off the bench in Northampton Town's 4-0 defeat in a third round tie in January, 1998.

Leicester made a mistake when they let Dixie McNeil leave the club. After his release in 1966, he went on to score 239 goals in the Football League in spells with Exeter City, Northampton, Lincoln City, Hereford United (twice) and Wrexham.

Pat Bonner is another player City really should have hung on to. He was between the posts for the Foxes during the 1975-76 FA Youth Cup campaign and had a career at the highest level with Celtic and Ireland.

Northern Ireland international Ian Stewart, formerly with Queens Park Rangers and Newcastle United, also didn't do enough in a couple of Central League games in 1988 to earn a contract with City.

Fans of a certain age may remember central defender Grant Brown making 16 appearances during the late 1980s. Up the A46 in Lincoln, he is regarded as one of the Imps' finest-ever players having made a club record 407 appearances.

DOUBLE TROUBLE

At the time of scribbling – December, 2008 – only ten teams have won the Football League championship and FA Cup double.

In 1962-63, Leicester City were on course to join a list that features Manchester United (1994, 1996, 1999), Arsenal (1971, 1998, 2002), Liverpool (1986), Tottenham Hotspur (1961), Aston Villa (1897) and Preston North End (1889).

City's 4-3 win over Manchester United at Filbert Street on April 16th, 1963, secured by Ken Keyworth's hat-trick, took them back to the top of the Division One table with just five games left in the season and Matt Gillies' team also had an FA Cup semi-final against Liverpool to look forward to 11 days later.

Incredibly, the Foxes took just one point from their remaining top-flight fixtures and ended the season fourth after four straight defeats. That was City's highest finish since 1928-29 when they finished runners-up behind Sheffield Wednesday and while their failed title challenge was a crushing disappointment, Mike Stringfellow's goal in the FA Cup semi-final at Hillsborough gave them the chance to lift the trophy for the first time.

City were making their third appearance in the showpiece final and were fancied to beat a Manchester United side who had spent most of the season battling against the drop from Division One.

Instead, a Leicester team that included new internationals Gordon Banks, Frank McLintock and Davie Gibson flopped. They were beaten

3-1 with Keyworth on target and that meant Leicester finished the season empty-handed having six weeks earlier been on course to lift two trophies.

ANOTHER ELITE GROUP

On the subject of elite groups... until May 4th, 2008, City were one of only ten clubs to have never played outside the top two divisions of English football.

All that changed when a goalless draw at Stoke City's Britannia Stadium wasn't enough to keep Ian Holloway's team in the Championship. Gareth McAuley was a whisker away from rescuing City with a second-half header that smacked against the woodwork, but a 3-2 victory for Southampton against Sheffield United on a dramatic afternoon meant the Foxes ended up being relegated alongside Colchester United and Scunthorpe United.

Ironically, the manager who masterminded Southampton's survival at the expense of City went on to become Leicester's next boss after Holloway left. Nigel Pearson was handed the task of leading City back into the Championship.

GOD IS A LEICESTER FAN

As with most clubs, Leicester City have the odd celebrity fan... and no supporter of any of them can be more odd than Foxes fan David Icke!

Icke, you may remember, went from presenting snooker on the telly to declaring himself to be God's spokesman on Earth. David Neilson, the actor who played Roy Cropper in Coronation Street, was born in Loughborough and supports City, while television chef Rustie Lee was a regular at Filbert Street.

Elsewhere in the world of showbiz, Leicester's leading bands have followed the Foxes. Leicester rockers Family were regulars at Filbert Street and on the cover of the band's live album, Roger Chapman is belting out an anthem bedecked in a classic 1970s City shirt.

Other bands have followed in the shirt-wearing tradition including rockers Kasabian with singer Tom Meighan packing his City shirt when he heads off on tour to promote the band's number one albums. The band's guitarist, Serge Pizzorno, had trials at Nottingham Forest as a teenager and remembers wearing his Leicester socks under Forest's. They are regularly spotted at the Walkers Stadium and when they can't make it, Tom is on the phone to his father every few minutes for updates on City.

In the early 1990s, indie hopes Blab Happy wore their team's colours on stage and of the latest bunch of Leicester bands, The Screening are City supporters. While, the man inside Filbert Fox is one of their biggest fans! Showaddywaddy produced ten top-ten singles, including a number one, and guitarist Trevor Oakes produced two sons who played for his favourite team. Scott and Stef both played for their home-town club and the latter picked up a League Cup winners' medal in 2000.

Boxing champion Rendall Munroe is another City fan. Munroe won the European super-bantamweight boxing title in March, 2008 with a points win over previously unbeaten Spanish puncher Kiko Martinez that propelled him into the top ten of the world rankings. His favourite football team were less successful and two months later, City were relegated to the third tier of English football for the first time.

Mark Selby, a finalist in the 2007 world snooker championships, is a City fan and fellow potter Willie Thorne would go to Filbert Street to perform the half-time draw when he wasn't pocketing 147s or down the bookies.

Rather disappointingly, David Gower, the former Leicestershire batsman regarded as possibly the most talented English cricketer of his generation, supports Nottingham Forest.

HE BANGS THE DRUMS

Leicester City's biggest supporter is very big indeed. Lee Jobber tips the scales at around 30 stones – hopefully less by the time you read this – and the matchday experience at the Walkers Stadium simply would not be the same without the sight and sound of him stripped to the waist belting a drum.

His topless tub thumping has made him a legend among City fans and has led to him being followed by television cameras and splashed all over national newspapers and magazines.

Lee, an affable, cheery man from Braunstone, could have been playing for City rather than supporting them. As a schoolboy, he was a promising goalkeeper on the club's books until a shattering injury ended his footballing ambitions when he was just 15 years old. He dived to save a penalty during training and the force of the shot smashed his wrist. Devastated, Lee headed to the pub for a few years and when he wasn't drowning his sorrows, he was cheering on City. Then he started taking his clothes off.

It all started on the opening day of the 2002-2003 season and City's Premier League clash with Southampton at the Walkers Stadium. Lee sat in the stands sweltering uncomfortably and after some encouragement from his friends, peeled off his shirt and spent the second half getting a sun tan while watching City chuck away a 2-0 lead.

"After the game," he remembered, "my mate said he would buy me a season ticket the following season if I didn't wear my shirt again for the rest of that campaign, so I agreed.

"He never did buy me that season ticket, but at the first game of the next season, I sat down and about ten people said: 'Come on, get your shirt off.' So I took it off and it's been off ever since."

Then came the drum.

During the 2006-2007 season, the club approached Lee and asked him to add to the atmosphere at home games by standing at the back of the Alliance & Leicester stand with his shirt off beating a large drum. Lee agreed and after sinking a few drinks for some courage, made his drumming debut – next to a bunch of Millwall fans!

"Three bangs and you're out of breath," they chanted. Lee had a giggle, got through it and has been drumming ever since. Jobber has gone on to appear on *Football's Hardest Away Days* on Sky One and applied for the manager's job at City during the wretched 2007-2008 season.

FORGOTTEN HERO

And the winner is… well, everyone already knew. Gary Lineker's 24 goals had helped Leicester City secure 15th place in the top flight in 1984-85, earned an England call-up and made him a transfer target for the country's biggest clubs. So he would surely end the season by being named the Leicester City Supporters' Club's Player of the Year?

But that trophy is missing from a collection that includes 80 England caps, the Golden Boot from the 1986 World Cup and a winner's medal from the European Cup Winners' Cup earned when he was with Barcelona. Instead, City's fans handed the Player of the Year award to a player forgotten by many supporters.

Andy Feeley, a robust, uncompromising defender and midfielder, walked off with the trophy. Fans were possibly too scared to vote against him because if they had handed out an award for Player Whose Pint You Really Don't Want to Spill, Feeley would have won that as well.

Put simply, Feeley was hard. Built like the proverbial outhouse and wearing a plaster cast on his right arm to hide tattoos he was less than fond of, he wasn't exactly afraid of confrontation and his jobs after leaving football included a spell as a prison officer in a unit for the criminally insane.

Feeley first came to prominence on August 18th, 1979 when he entered the record books as the youngest captain in Football League history by leading out home-town club Hereford United against York City – aged just 17. But a fiery temperament and injuries meant there were fears his early promise would be unfulfilled.

Feeley ended up drifting into non-league football with Trowbridge – where his manager was Alan Birchenall! 'The Birch', a popular member of City's 1970s side, recommended Feeley to Gordon Milne and he was impressed enough to hand Andy his debut at Old Trafford in front of 39,473 fans in March, 1984.

The following season, Feeley made 41 appearances in all competitions to pip the soon-to-be-departing Lineker for the Player of the Year award and added 26 more in 1985-86 as City escaped the drop with victory over Newcastle United on the final day of the season.

City would have stood a better chance of securing a fifth successive season in the top flight had Feeley not been ruled out for the last two months of the 1986-87 campaign with a knee injury.

He left in the summer after rejecting a new deal and ended his career with Brentford and Bury.

THE ENTERTAINER

He loved Elvis Presley and for five glorious years, Frank Worthington was the king of Filbert Street.

Worthington left fans breathless with his skills on the pitch, broke hearts off the pitch and was undeniably the biggest personality of a Leicester City team packed with them.

He scored 78 goals in his 239 appearances for City and earned eight England caps – scoring twice – while starring for a flamboyant team put together by Jimmy Bloomfield. Worthington only ended up at Filbert Street because of a failed medical!

He was set to sign for Liverpool until that misfortune ended their interest and Bloomfield stepped in to sign him from Huddersfield Town in August, 1972 for a £100,000 fee that would prove to be a bargain.

'Wortho' made a goalscoring debut for the Foxes at Old Trafford as George Best grabbed Manchester United's goal in a 1-1 draw. With the talents of Keith Weller and Len Glover helping carve out openings for him, Worthington ended his first season at City with ten goals and added 20 more in 1973-74 as Leicester finished ninth in the top flight and reached the semi-finals of the FA Cup. At the end of the season, he was called up for England and grabbed his first goal for his country in his third appearance, a 2-2 draw with Argentina at Wembley.

Worthington only made eight appearances for his country, but the goals kept coming for the Foxes and it was a surprise to most supporters when

boss Frank McLintock decided to sell their hero to Bolton Wanderers in September, 1977. His final appearance for Leicester came in a 3-0 defeat at home to Nottingham Forest and he went on to become the top flight's leading scorer in the 1978-79 season with a 24-goal haul for the Trotters.

Worthington was soon on the move again and after making his debut for Birmingham City against Leicester, he made a goal-scoring farewell to Filbert Street in November, 1983. Frank, still good enough to play in the top flight around a decade after his pomp with Leicester, lined up against City for Southampton and found the target in a 2-1 defeat in front of a crowd of 14,181.

He was warmly received by City fans and his admirers at the ground that night included Gary Lineker, who grabbed Leicester's winner after Alan Smith had opened the scoring. Worthington returned to Leicestershire as player manager of Hinckley Town in 1990 which attracted a few misty-eyed City fans through the turnstiles.

QUE SERA, SERA

Back then, nobody with any brains wanted to go to Cambridge. It was an intimidating place and you were likely to leave there bruised, battered and empty-handed. At the Abbey Stadium in the university city, all the punting was directed by Cambridge United boss John Beck, who set about masterminding a revolution with a bit of help from a player born and raised in Leicester.

Dion Dublin's talents escaped the attention of City's scouts – despite growing up just around the corner from Filbert Street – and after a spell at Norwich City, he launched his career at Cambridge. They were in the basement division when he went there and Beck's bruising, unconventional tactics took them to back-to-back promotions and the quarter-finals of the FA Cup in successive seasons.

Leicester were also enjoying something of an upturn in fortunes at the start of the 1991-92 season and in September, a 3-0 win over Blackburn Rovers at Filbert Street took them up to third in the Division One table and meant they travelled to Cambridge for a Sunday afternoon fixture flushed with a confidence that was then comprehensively battered out of them.

City were on the receiving end of a 5-1 thumping at the Abbey Stadium with Colin Gordon grabbing the consolation. Dublin and future City legend Steve Claridge got two goals apiece for the home side. Leicester went on to avenge the loss with a 2-1 victory at Filbert Street the following April that was secured by goals from Tommy Wright and Phil Gee and kept the Foxes second in the table with two games remaining in the season.

Defeats against Charlton Athletic and Newcastle United meant City had to settle for the play-offs rather than automatic promotion and a two-legged semi-final against Cambridge. They returned from the Abbey Stadium with a 1-1 draw after the first leg which set up an unforgettable night at Filbert Street with City aiming to reach Wembley for the first time since the 1969 FA Cup Final defeat against Manchester City. Tommy Wright opened the scoring late in the first half when he got to a near-post corner and stabbed the ball into the roof of the net. Cambridge fell apart after the break.

Wright added another and further strikes from Steve Thompson, Kevin Russell and Ian Ormondroyd secured a stunning 5-0 win that sent the majority of the 21,054 crowd wild with delight, and the Foxes back to Wembley – to face Blackburn Rovers – after an absence of 23 years.

REDS SING THE BLUES

Liverpool have lifted more trophies than any other English club. They also have a bogey team – and it's Leicester City. For more than four decades, City have made a habit of chucking a spanner in the works for the Merseyside giants and perhaps the most remarkable of all Leicester's performances against Liverpool came in the 1980-81 season.

Jock Wallace's team, promoted to the top flight as Second Division champions, had started the season with back-to-back defeats and then stunned the Reds at Filbert Street through Andy Peake's long-range shot and a strike from Martin Henderson. City went on to complete an astonishing double in January, 1981 by ending Liverpool's 85-match unbeaten run at Anfield.

Leicester had lost their previous five games, but ripped up the formbook with Jim Melrose bagging both goals in a 2-1 win. Liverpool's goal came through an Alan Young own goal. City were still relegated at the end of the season.

Leicester also completed a league double over the Reds in the 1962-63 season when City were chasing both the Division One championship and FA Cup and they handed Liverpool a double dose of league misery again in the 1964-65 campaign.

REDS DRAWING

City produced a pair of determined performances against Liverpool in 1983-84. Mark Wallington saved a penalty from Graeme Souness to secure a 2-2 draw at Anfield and the sides fought out a thrilling 3-3 draw at Filbert Street later in the season.

The following season, Alan Smith and Gary Lineker got the goals for Gordon Milne's team in a 2-1 win at Liverpool.

THREE ON THE BOUNCE

Under Martin O'Neill, City won at Anfield for three successive seasons. They were 2-1 winners in the second game of the 1997-98 season through goals from Matt Elliott and Graham Fenton and the following season, former Everton striker Ian Marshall was City's last-gasp match winner on Merseyside. City followed that in May, 2000 with a 2-0 win at Anfield thanks to strikes from Tony Cottee and Phil Gilchrist. Leicester's winning run at Anfield came to an end the following season with a 1-0 defeat – the goal scorer was former City striker Emile Heskey.

IN THE BIG TIME

All around the streets of Leicester, people were united in joy. Men, women and children sang, danced and embraced.

No, I'm not describing the scenes on the day this publication hit the city's bookshops. It was the sight that greeted Leicester Fosse's players, though, when they stepped out of the city's train station on London Road on Monday April 27th, 1908 having earlier that day secured a 1-0 win at Stoke City that took them into the top flight of English football for the first time in the club's 24-year history.

The players spent hours trying to weave their way home through the rejoicing throng of fans that had gathered on London Road and Granby Street, so if you thought the traffic around there these days is bad, think again.

Fosse had gone into the season confident they could secure a top-two finish and a place among the elite. The club announced record season-ticket sales that brought in £1,167 and ground improvements increased the capacity at Filbert Street to 22,000. The club also signed new players including forwards Jimmy Donnelly and Percy Humphreys and set about climbing out of Division Two.

They were beaten only once in the opening 11 games and after Humphreys was allowed to move to Chelsea for a fee of £350, the arrival of Fred Shinton in a deal from West Bromwich Albion helped kick-start the promotion challenge. Fosse were eighth in the table going into the home date with Blackpool on February 15th, 1908 and Humphreys got both goals in a 2-1 win that started a club-record run of seven straight victories.

The winning run included a 5-1 thrashing of Bradford City – who would go on to be crowned champions – and came to an abrupt end with a 5-1 defeat at Fulham on April 4th. The battle for the second promotion place went down to the final day of the season. Bradford had already secured the championship and Fosse were level on points with promotion rivals Oldham Athletic, but had a better goal average than the Latics.

That victory at Stoke would guarantee promotion for Fosse and they claimed maximum points through a Tommy Shanks strike. He netted from close range after Shinton's shot had been blocked by the Stoke custodian. Fosse keeper Horace Bailey, who had recently been capped by England, was in sparkling form at the other end of the pitch to ensure Leicester held on to their advantage and ended the club's wait for top-flight football.

MATT FINISH

It's what the old place would have wanted. In May, 2002, Matt Piper, born in Leicester and a life-long Foxes fan, netted the last goal at the Filbert Street ground where he was once a ball boy. His diving header secured a 2-1 win over Tottenham Hotspur and ensured there wasn't a dry eye in the house at the final whistle.

Sadly, whoever was writing Piper's scripts ran out of ink after that. He was sold to Sunderland for £3.5 million to help ease City's financial problems and then had to retire in the summer of 2007 after undergoing an incredible 16 operations on his knees and ankles.

Peter Shilton and Gary Lineker also made their boyhood dreams come true by playing for City. In May, 1963, Shilton stood behind the goal at Wembley watching Leicester lose the FA Cup Final to Manchester United and six years later, he was between the posts for the showpiece game as Manchester City lifted the trophy and sent Gary Lineker sobbing all the way home.

Graham Cross was another who grew up supporting City and went on to play for them many times. As a seven-year-old, he would sit on the wall in front of the Popular Side terrace and cheer on the likes of Arthur Rowley and a decade later he made his debut for his home-town club. Cross went on to play in two FA Cup Finals, two League Cup Finals and set a club record of 599 appearances that probably would have been more if he hadn't been so good at cricket! His decision to help Leicestershire win their first County Championship in 1975 rather than report back for pre-season training wasn't well received at Filbert Street and spelled the beginning of the end for him at City.

Andy Peake grew up in Market Harborough supporting City and went on to make more than 150 appearances for his team. He is remembered for a spectacular goal against Division One champions Liverpool at Filbert Street in August, 1980.

Richard Smith's claim to fame is that he grabbed the goal that handed City their first win in the FA Cup for seven years. Smith, a regular in the

Spion Kop as a teenager, netted the last-minute winner against Crystal Palace in the third round in January, 1991.

Another regular in Brian Little's first season at Filbert Street was a life-long City fan. Nicky Platnauer made no secret of his boyhood devotion to City when he joined the club.

SOCCER'S NICEST STRIKERS

Alan Smith was leaving Leicester City – and he was staying at Leicester City. His goals for City during four successive seasons in the top flight meant it was no surprise when it was announced in March, 1987 that Smith would be joining former strike partner Gary Lineker on the way out of Filbert Street after agreeing an £800,000 switch to Arsenal.

The deal allowed Smith to stay at City for the rest of the season as Bryan Hamilton's team battled against relegation and that arrangement put him in a strange position when his two teams came face to face at Highbury the following month.

Smith lined up for City in the 4-1 defeat and was cheered by both sets of supporters! There were only Leicester tears at the end of the season, however. A goalless draw at Oxford United couldn't keep them up and at the final whistle, Smith peeled his shirt off and threw it into the hordes of Leicester fans behind the goal.

Smith had arrived from non-league Alvechurch in the summer of 1982 and for three seasons, Smith and Lineker formed arguably the most feared strikeforce in the country and definitely the nicest!

Lineker was never booked or sent off throughout his career, while Smith picked up just one booking in his 217 games for City and when the referee reached for his notebook, he apparently sighed: "There goes my disciplinary record."

Smith had much more to be proud of. A tall, elegant striker willing to chase and harry, he bagged 13 goals in his first season as Gordon Milne's team pipped Fulham for the third promotion spot and that haul included a belter in the 5-0 demolition of Wolverhampton Wanderers that City's excitable programme editor described as "one of the best goals seen at Filbert Street for many years".

The following season, Smith, Lineker and Lynex bagged 49 top-flight goals between them and after Lineker's departure at the end of 1984-85 it was left to Smith to spearhead City's attack for two seasons. He left City after scoring 84 goals in all competitions and enjoyed much more success at Highbury. Smith scored one goal and set up the other as the Gunners snatched the Division One title in the dying seconds of the 1988-89 season, briefly played alongside Lineker for England and volleyed home the winner in the 1994 European Cup Winners' Cup Final against Parma. He retired through injury at the age of just 32 and went on to work in the media.

LET'S HAVE A COFFEE

There are two books – and now a page in this one – dedicated to the wit and wisdom of a former Leicester City manager – and it's not Gordon Milne. Ian Holloway, appointed City's third manager of the season in November, 2007, would keep reporters waiting until past their deadline before coming into the press room and reeling off priceless soundbytes to leave hardened hacks sniggering.

He did just that after only his third game in charge at City – a 2-1 defeat at home to Southampton in December, 2007 that kept Leicester in trouble near the bottom of the Championship. Holloway was unhappy that a section of Leicester fans had targeted striker Carl Cort for stick and said: "To the people who booed – boo to you!"

His decision to quit Plymouth Argyle to take the job at Leicester incensed Pilgrims fans and they vented their anger during their side's 1-0 win at the Walkers Stadium in February, 2008.

Holloway shrugged: "Apparently, it's my fault that the *Titanic* sank." Later in the season, he called Sheffield United striker Billy Sharp a "little turkey" after he won the penalty that sent City on their way to a 3-0 defeat at Bramall Lane. Sadly, the quote that stays in the memory from Holloway's six months at the Walkers Stadium was made as the season headed towards its climax.

"I don't want to be the only manager to have taken Leicester to the division below the Championship," he said. Unfortunately, that is on his CV. Holloway can hardly take full responsibility for City's relegation, but he was in charge when they dropped out of the top two divisions of English football for the first time following the goalless draw at Stoke City.

OLLY'S FAMOUS WORDS

Holloway's most famous quote came after he had steered Queens Park Rangers to an "ugly" win at Chesterfield. He said: "To put it in gentleman's terms, if you've been out for a night and you're looking for a young lady and you pull one, some weeks they're good looking and some weeks they're not the best. Our performance today would have been not the best looking bird, but at least we got her in the taxi. She weren't the best looking lady we ended up taking home, but she was very pleasant and very nice, so thanks very much, let's have a coffee."

IT'S A FUNNY OLD GAME

In September, 1933, Burnley-based referee H. E. Hull was set to take charge of the top-flight match between Leicester and Chelsea at Filbert Street. He found the dressing room, changed into his kit, walked out onto the pitch and then noticed something unusual. There were too many players and the ball was the wrong shape. Hull had turned up at Welford Road by mistake!

Realising he was at a rugby union fixture rather than a football match, Hull headed to Filbert Street where City and Chelsea drew 1-1. The point gained took Leicester up to third in Division One.

OOOPS!

Leicester Fosse reserves travelled to their Sheffield Wednesday counterparts for a Midland League fixture in 1908-09 and ended up doing it all over again after a refereeing blunder led to the game being replayed in its entirety. The referee awarded Fosse a penalty in the dying moments of the game – and then blew the final whistle before they had the chance to take it! That led to complaints from Fosse and the game being played again.

REF NEEDS GLASSES

A piece of refereeing incompetence denied Arthur Chandler a goal against Middlesbrough at Filbert Street in September, 1924. The officials didn't spot that Channy's shot had hit the stanchion in the goal before the ball bounced back into play and no goal was awarded. Not that it mattered much. Although the game finished goalless, City went on to win the Division Two title and Chandler ended up with 32 league goals. He netted 273 times in his City career to be the club's record goalscorer.

KNOCKOUT BLOW

A linesman was in the firing line when Leicester met Wolves at Filbert Street in April, 1934. A stray clearance knocked him unconscious during a match also remembered for a double sending off. Arthur Lochhead and Wolves defender Crook were both given their marching orders in a game that finished 1-1. Perhaps there was some ill feeling between the pair following the sides' meeting at Molineux the previous day! Both games ended in 1-1 draws with Arthur Maw grabbing the Foxes goal in both fixtures.

STICKS

It was November 23rd, 1994 and Leicester City needed a hero. Step forward – and try not to fall over – Ian Ormondroyd. These were desperate times. City were in disarray. They were rooted to the foot of the Premiership after four straight defeats and the previous day, manager Brian Little had announced his resignation while having one eye on the job at Aston Villa. On the morning of the game, John Gregory decided he was off as well and that left Allan Evans in charge for the visit of Arsenal to Filbert Street. Incredibly, City ran out 2-1 winners against the Gunners in front of 20,774 supporters, and Ormondroyd was the hero.

At least for a few weeks. The joyless souls at the Premiership Panel decided that the game's decisive strike was a David Seaman own goal and Ormondroyd was denied what would have been the only Premiership goal of his career. The striker only found the target 12 times in 96 City appearances – celebrating each one with the unco-ordinated joy of a schoolboy on the last day of term before the summer holidays – and there were some crucial efforts among them. He was on target in the second leg of the play-off semi-final at Portsmouth in May, 1993 to help send City through to Wembley and the following season he was the last-gasp hero in a dramatic 4-4 draw against Watford at Filbert Street.

Ormondroyd also had a hand in the goal that took City into the Premier League in May, 1994. His header in the closing minutes of the Division One play-off final at Wembley was saved by Derby keeper Martin Taylor and Steve Walsh was there to tap home the rebound and send City back into the top tier. The lanky striker had joined City from the Rams along with strike partner Phil Gee in March, 1992 in a deal which sent Paul Kitson in the opposite direction. The gangly hitman with the physique of a dieting pipe cleaner was soon suffering frustration in front of goal.

In his second game for Leicester, Ormondroyd had two first-half goals ruled out at promotion rivals Ipswich Town and then fell over his own feet later in the match when he looked to lead a City counter attack! He was later used as a left winger – despite standing a towering 6ft 4ins. tall – and earned cult status among Leicester fans before rejoining home-town club Bradford City in the summer of 1995 following City's relegation from the Premiership.

ALL TOGETHER NOW

As sung by Louis Armstrong, Billie Holliday… and Pen Three of the Spion Kop at Filbert Street! The song adopted as Leicester City's anthem was originally a hit in the depths of the Great Depression in the 1920s. Designed to lift the spirits in such desperate times, When You're Smiling has had a similar effect on City fans.

Then again, the song has also been heard in happier times. It was written by Shay, Fisher and Goodwin and was originally released by Louis Armstrong in September, 1929. When You're Smiling was re-released in 1932 and then 1956. Billie Holliday also recorded a version of the song. Not sure that either Armstrong or Holliday used to waggle their fingers when singing the song's title, however.

First heard on the Filbert Street terraces around the time of Holliday's version going into the charts, When You're Smiling made something of a comeback around the start of the 1990s when Brian Little led City's revival after several years of struggle. All together now...

> When you're smiling, when you're smiling
> The whole world smiles with you
> And when you're laughing, when you're laughing
> The sun comes shining through
>
> But when you're crying, you bring on the rain
> So stop you're crying, be happy again
> 'Cause when you're smiling, when you're smiling
> The whole world smiles with you.

Leicester supporters also have a unique version of another football anthem. To the tune of We're On The March With Ally's Army from Scotland's 1978 World Cup bid, it goes something like this...

> Bring on the Sunderland and Arsenal
> Bring on Scousers by the score
> Barcelona, Real Madrid
> They all make a mighty bid
> But they won't beat Leicester any more

BLONDES HAVE MORE FUN

Tottenham Hotspur won the Worthington Cup, Leicester City suffered last-gasp heartbreak, but all the headlines were about Robbie Savage. Just the way he likes it then? Martin O'Neill took his City side back to Wembley for the third time in four seasons in March, 1999 to face Spurs and they faced them without Frank Sinclair. He was dropped on the eve of the game for a breach of club discipline and that controversy was nothing compared to what followed when the game got under way.

City probably created the better chances in the first half and then came the game's flashpoint. In the 63rd minute, Savage, City's chief mischief maker and pantomime villain, took a tumble after a collision with Spurs defender Justin Edinburgh. Referee Terry Heilbron gave Edinburgh his marching orders and Spurs' players, clearly incensed by what they believed to be play-acting on Savage's part, set about exacting retribution. As tempers reached boiling point, Savage was the victim of several crunching tackles and while he survived, City didn't.

The game was in its final minute and heading for extra time when Steffen Iversen pulled the ball back from the right-hand byeline, City keeper Kasey Keller got a hand to it, but Allan Nielsen was perfectly placed to head home the winner. The late drama was hard on City defender Rob Ullathorne. As he had done two years earlier in the final against Middlesbrough, O'Neill had handed one of his players a man-marking job and Ullathorne's shackling of David Ginola would have surely earned him the man-of-the-match award had it not been for Nielsen's late match winner. Not that anybody seemed to notice Ullathorne or even that Spurs had lifted the cup. The national press were more concerned in condemning Savage following Edinburgh's sending off.

Savage, more determined than most blondes to prove that they do indeed have more fun, stunned nobody in particular when he later admitted that Edinburgh hadn't made contact in the incident that led to his dismissal. If nothing else, his honesty about his dishonesty was refreshing.

City's defeat at Wembley was hard on Tony Cottee. He had netted five times in previous rounds – including strikes in both legs of the semi-final win over Sunderland – and the loss meant he had to wait to claim his first winner's medal. A couple of weeks after the loss to Spurs, Cottee was on target in a 2-0 win for City at White Hart Lane to register his 200th goal in the Football League.

SPLASHING THE CASH

Leicester Fosse's first season in their now traditional blue and white strip was in 1903-1904 – and they celebrated by finishing bottom of the table! That meant Fosse had to apply for re-election and they survived after the Football League put the decision to the vote.

Fosse responded to this narrow escape by splashing out their first transfer fee at the end of the season. They forked out £300 to bring former England international centre-half Billy Bannister to the club from Woolwich Arsenal. Three years later, Fosse doubled that record outlay to sign another former England international. Percy Humphries made the move from East Midlands rivals Notts County for £600.

The club's first four-figure signing came in June, 1923 and proved to be money well spent. City signed Arthur Chandler from Queens Park Rangers for a £3,000 fee and he went on to be the club's record goalscorer. City broke the £10,000 barrier in July, 1950 when they paid £14,000 to sign Arthur Rowley from Fulham and another transfer from the Cottagers 18 years later put Leicester into the record books. The fee of £150,000 they paid to bring in Allan Clarke from Fulham was a British transfer record and 12 months later 'Sniffer' was on his way to Leeds United in a move that rewrote that best mark. He left Filbert Street for a fee of £165,000.

The deal that brought Roger Davies to Filbert Street in December, 1977 became Leicester's record transfer. Davies joined from Belgian club Bruges for £250,000 in December, 1977, but couldn't keep Frank McLintock's side in the top flight. Alan Young and Jim Melrose were signed for the same fee from Oldham Athletic and Partick Thistle, respectively, and City set a new club record transfer when Bryan Hamilton signed Steve Moran from Southampton in September, 1986. A year later, Mike Newell arrived from Luton Town for £350,000 and that remained the biggest transfer fee paid by Leicester for six and a half years.

Ian Ormondroyd and Lee Philpott also joined for £350,000 – and then the club paid out £360,000 for Mark Blake in March, 1994. Three months later, Mark Draper became Leicester's first £1 million signing when the midfielder joined from Notts County for £1.25 million. Frank Sinclair became City's first £2 million signing when he joined from Chelsea for £2.05 million and Darren Eadie and Gary Rowett both commanded £3 million fees.

Ade Akinbiyi was a £5 million signing from Wolverhampton Wanderers in July, 2000 and that remains the club's record signing.

GONE IN SIXTY SECONDS

Leicester City supporters celebrated, danced and then their hearts sank – all in the space of 60 breathless seconds. City thought they had drawn level against Wolverhampton Wanderers in their first appearance in the FA Cup Final in April, 1949 and a few seconds later, their challenge for the trophy was effectively over.

They weren't given much chance going into the game. Leicester were scrapping for survival at the bottom of Division Two and were underdogs against their top-flight opponents. In the first half, they lived down to that billing as Jesse Pye's goal double put Wolves on course to lift the trophy.

That was no surprise after City's preparations had been wrecked in the weeks before the game. Don Revie, a key figure in getting Leicester to Wembley, had been ruled out after a nose injury that led to a near fatal loss of blood and the makeshift line-up included full-back Jimmy Harrison playing at centre-forward and Jack Lee taking on the unfamiliar inside-forward role. Unsurprisingly, they were on the receiving end in the first half and then two minutes after the re-start, City were back in the game after boss John Duncan made changes to his forward line during the interval. Wolves goalkeeper Bert Williams couldn't hold on to Ken Chisholm's powerful drive and Mal Griffiths turned the loose ball home to hand City a lifeline.

The outcome of the game was then settled in the space of a few seconds. Leicester thought they were level in the 64th minute when Chisholm steered the ball into the net from the tightest of angles after good work from Griffiths. But the effort was ruled out for a marginal offside spotted by the linesman and with City still shell-shocked, Wolves went up the other end of the pitch and Sammy Smyth's stunning solo goal put the game beyond the Foxes.

City had good reason for optimism going into their first game at Wembley having caused a sensation in the semi-finals. The draw pitted Leicester, who were 20th in Division Two at the time, with Division One leaders and eventual champions Portsmouth. City, making only their second appearance at the semi-final stage, were 3-1 winners with Revie the architect of a famous victory. He netted twice and Chisholm got the other goal as City ripped up the formbook to silence the Pompey chimes.

There was a happy ending to the season for City and their supporters as they preserved their Division Two status on the final day.

CAN YOU SEE US ON THE BOX?

Leicester City's first appearance in a Football League game broadcast live on terrestrial television had a starring role from 'The Hot Dog Kid'.

City goalkeeper Carl Muggleton suffered a slipped disc in the warm up before the clash with Wolverhampton Wanderers in September, 1992 and that meant 19-year-old Russell Hoult had to quickly polish off his pre-match meal and take his place between the posts for his Foxes debut.

Hoult, raised in Whitwick, showed why he had been named City's Young Player of the Year in 1991 with a man-of-the-match display in a goalless draw. Hoult went on to concede only one goal in his opening five league appearances for City – and then shipped seven in a League Cup hammering at Sheffield Wednesday.

City made their television debut in the FA Cup Final in 1949 – but not many fans tuned in to watch the 3-1 defeat against Wolverhampton Wanderers. Apparently, there were only 35 television sets in Leicester and the surrounding district capable of receiving the live broadcast.

Six years later came the first broadcast of highlights from a City game at Filbert Street. The BBC programme *Sportsview* screened the best bits of Leicester's Division Two clash with Swansea City – and there were plenty of them in a 6-1 win for the Foxes. Willie Gardiner was City's hat-trick hero and the other goals came from Mal Griffiths, Johnny Morris and Arthur Rowley.

The *Match of the Day* cameras came to Filbert Street for the first time in October, 1964 to capture all the drama as City edged out Nottingham Forest 3-2. Mike Stringfellow was Leicester's match-winner with a header five minutes from the end, but goalkeeper Gordon Banks was the hero. He received a boot in the face from Colin Appleton in the first half and commentator Kenneth Wolstenholme of "some people are on the pitch" fame later described City fans as "rather justifiably booing Addison". Billy Hodgson put City ahead and less than a minute after Forest levelled, Colin Appleton restored the advantage after Bobby Svarc had been upended. Forest equalised again before Stringfellow had the final word.

STAYING UP

Think of The Great Escape and you probably think of Steve McQueen, secret tunnels and motor bikes. Unless you're from Leicester, that is.

In that case, you probably think of Saturday May 11th, 1991 and a match between Leicester City and Oxford United at Filbert Street that the Foxes had to win to avoid the drop into the third tier of English football for the first time in their history. It had been a wretched season for City. An opening-day win over Bristol Rovers at Filbert Street was followed by seven straight defeats – including a 6-0 humbling at Middlesbrough – and with the team in desperate relegation trouble and crowd figures dwindling below 10,000, manager David Pleat was sacked at the end of January.

Gordon Lee was appointed caretaker boss and although there were signs of improvement, City showed all the survival instincts of a suicidal lemming as the relegation battle entered the closing weeks. They threw away a lead at relegation rivals West Bromwich Albion, losing 2-1, and back-to-back defeats against Swindon Town and Ipswich Town meant the Foxes' fate would be determined on the final day of the season. City took on Oxford United knowing they had to better West Bromwich

Albion's result at Bristol Rovers to stay in Division Two and the early news from Twerton Park was not encouraging. Rovers had a player sent off in the 24th minute to settle City's nerves. A corner fell to Tony James and he scooped the ball into the roof of the net from close range to give Leicester a priceless lead.

City continued to dominate and the Baggies could only draw 1-1 at Bristol Rovers to ensure Leicester stayed up at their expense. Along with Bristol Rovers' ten men, James was the hero, but City were saved as much by the Football League's ruling at the start of the season that only two teams would be relegated from Division Two rather than three. Had three teams gone down, City would have suffered the drop. Forty-two years earlier, Jack Lee had been City's hero when City had a similar escape. In May, 1949 – just seven days after losing the FA Cup Final against Wolverhampton Wanderers at Wembley – they needed a point at Cardiff City to survive and Lee popped up with the crucial equaliser at Ninian Park.

THE SWEET FA CUP

Leicester City reached the semi-finals of the FA Cup for the first time in their history in 1934. Then it all went wrong.

City's clash with Portsmouth at St. Andrew's on March 17th, 1934 attracted a then-record attendance of 66,544 to Birmingham City's ground and the Foxes had happy memories of the venue. In the fifth round of the competition, they had been 2-1 winners at Birmingham with Arthur Chandler grabbing both goals. Chandler had then been City's marksman in the 1-0 win at Preston North End in the quarter-finals that took the Foxes through to the last four for the first time. Their debut at the semi-final stage was ruined by misfortune.

City fell behind early on while distracted by fans spilling onto the touchline after fencing collapsed behind the goal and worse followed with defender Sandy Wood being left dazed and with a broken nose following a collision with a photographer. Andy Lochhead did score for City in the first half, but it was Pompey striker John Weddle who grabbed the headlines. He had been in the Portsmouth line-up that was on the receiving end of a 10-0 thrashing at Filbert Street in October,

1928 and gained some revenge for that humiliation with a hat-trick in the 4-1 win that ended City's Wembley hopes.

48 YEARS LATER...

Leicester City didn't exactly have the best of luck in the 1982 FA Cup semi-final either. The good news was they were playing just up the road at Villa Park, so it was a bit like a home fixture; the bad news was they had to face favourites Tottenham Hotspur. Jock Wallace's team had beaten top-flight opposition on the way to the last four – Alan Young's double powered them to a 3-1 win over Southampton in the third round – but Spurs were the cup holders and could call upon the talents of Ossie Ardiles and Glenn Hoddle.

They really didn't need any help from Lady Luck. City fell behind to Garth Crooks' first-half strike and then Leicester were hit by a double blow. Tommy Williams was carried off with a broken leg and Ian Wilson scored a spectacular own goal to put the game beyond the Foxes. His attempted back pass to Mark Wallington looped over his head and dropped into the net to complete a miserable afternoon for City.

CHEAT FELL OVER

To Leicester City supporters, he was a diver, he was a cheat. Worse still, in July, 1993 David Speedie was a Leicester player. The signing of the Scot by manager Brian Little divided supporters who remembered the Division One play-off final in May, 1992.

Twenty-three years after City's FA Cup Final defeat against Manchester City, they were back at Wembley to face Blackburn Rovers with a place in the newly-formed Premier League at stake. The prospect of being able to spend Jack Walker's millions tempted Kenny Dalglish to the Ewood Park hot seat after previously quitting the manager's job at former club Liverpool. City's side had cost considerably less to put together and although five weeks before the play-off final Little's cut-price heroes had been 1-0 winners at Ewood Park through Kevin Russell's goal, they were still fancied to suffer a fifth defeat in five visits to Wembley.

The game was decided in the dying moments of the first half. Rovers striker Speedie took a theatrical tumble following a challenge by Steve Walsh and referee George Courtney was more impressed by his theatrics than City's skipper and the thousands of Leicester fans among the crowd of 68,147. He pointed to the penalty spot and to make matters worse for City fans, it was former Foxes striker Mike Newell who stepped up to convert past goalkeeper Carl Muggleton. City piled on the pressure in the second half and had a couple of efforts scrambled off the goal line. Blackburn counter-attacked in the closing minutes.

Muggleton's challenge sent Mark Atkins crashing for a more clear-cut penalty, but this time City's goalkeeper picked the right way to dive and kept out Newell's spot kick. There was still time for a City equaliser, but it didn't come and Leicester were resigned to spending a sixth successive season outside the top flight. At the start of the campaign, Little and City's fans would have settled for an appearance in the play-off final having narrowly escaped the drop into the third tier of English football for the first time in May, 1991.

They claimed 13 points from the opening 15 available and a spell of five successive wins in April – including wins over Blackburn and Cambridge United – cemented their play-off place. City finished fifth and booked their trip to Wembley by beating Cambridge over two legs in the play-off semi-finals. They followed a 1-1 draw at the Abbey Stadium with a 5-0 pasting on an unforgettable night at a sunny and euphoric Filbert Street.

BRUNO

A decade after Gary Lineker left The City of Leicester School, another future England international walked through the school gates. As a teenager, Ian Thompson was a match-winner for England Schools at Filbert Street, joined Leicester City and even appeared on a team photograph. Sadly, the powerfully-built striker's promise was unfulfilled.

Thompson, a talented cricketer like Lineker, was hit by injuries and after his release by City without making a first-team appearance, he ended up playing in local football – including a spell at Shepshed Dynamo. Emile

Heskey was also still a pupil at the Evington School when he made his international breakthrough by winning caps for England under-16s and he was just two months past his 17th birthday when handed his City debut in the 2-0 Premier League defeat at Queens Park Rangers in March, 1995.

His first goal came the following season. Heskey stepped off the bench to get the winner against Norwich City and keep Mark McGhee's side on top of the table. Heskey went on to secure Martin O'Neill's first win as City manager in the 3-2 success at Wolverhampton Wanderers. He was on target twice in the win against the club McGhee joined after quitting City. Heskey made an instant impact in the Premier League on City's return to the top flight. He netted both goals in a 2-1 win over Southampton in the first home game of the campaign – including a rampaging run and shot that was an early contender for Goal of the Season.

'Bruno' ended the season with a Coca-Cola Cup winner's medal. His late equaliser forced a replay in the final with Middlesbrough and Steve Claridge grabbed the only goal at Hillsborough. Heskey added another League Cup winner's medal in 2000 and the final victory over Tranmere Rovers came just a few days after he had marked his first full appearance for England with a man-of-the-match performance in a goalless draw against Argentina at Wembley.

A few days after the win over Tranmere – and a starring role alongside hat-trick hero Stan Collymore in a 5-2 demolition of Sunderland at Filbert Street – Heskey was off to Liverpool in an £11 million deal that was the third biggest signing by a British club at the time. Emile ended his first full season at Anfield with a 22-goal haul as the Reds won the FA, League and UEFA Cups and was one of England's heroes in the 5-1 win against Germany in Munich in September, 2001. He scored the last goal in the romp.

RAISING A SMILE

The 1980s was a dark decade for English football. The disasters at Heysel and Hillsborough made it ugly times for the beautiful game, so up popped fanzines to put a smile back on the face of football. These unofficial publications gave fans the chance to voice opinions that the club programme and local paper would have been unlikely to print.

The title *For Fox Sake* gives you some idea of the mood of Leicester supporters when the first issue appeared during the 1990-91 battle against the drop into the third tier of English football. *The Fox* also came out around the same time.

An early issue of *The Fox* had Leicester boss David Pleat on its cover with his head in his hands in the dug out with the caption: "Calling International Rescue". The mix of well-written nostalgia, humour and cartoons has made *The Fox* a good seller among supporters and when City enjoyed their early 1990s revival under Brian Little, the publication's replica shirts from the 1960s and 1970s were often spotted on the terraces. *The Fox* remains the only City fanzine, but there have been a few others.

Where's The Money Gone?

…came out during another troubled time for City – and the title was even chanted at Filbert Street as Leicester crashed out of the Premier League in 1994-95. The supporters who put together *WTMG* wanted to know why a club that had brought in funds by the sale of star players including Gary Lineker and Alan Smith could not sustain a top-flight football team or keep their manager following the departures of Brian Little and Mark McGhee in the space of 12 turbulent months. The pages of the fanzine bristled with humour and resentment and it picked up several awards from football magazines. *WTMG* disappeared when City started their revival under Martin O'Neill. There wasn't anything to be angry about any more.

When You're Smiling

There was another City fanzine that came out around the same time as *Where's The Money Gone?* Named *When You're Smiling* after the City supporters' anthem, it was backed by Foxes Against Racism and along with the usual features, it also gave publicity to local bands before disappearing after a few issues.

THE LEGEND NOBODY WANTED

Leicester City's top ten all-time leading goalscorers

273	Arthur Chandler
265	Arthur Rowley
156	Ernie Hine
117	Derek Hines
114	Arthur Lochhead
113	George Dewis
103	Gary Lineker
97	Jack Lee
97	Mike Stringfellow
95	Johnny Duncan

Unbelievable as it may seem now, the arrival at Filbert Street of the player who went on to become the leading goalscorer in Football League history caused outrage among Leicester City supporters.

Arthur Rowley tops the Football League's scoring charts with 433 goals – 54 more than second-placed Dixie Dean – and he scored 251 of those for City with another 14 coming in the FA Cup. Rowley came to Leicester in the summer of June, 1950 as a replacement for popular, Sileby-born forward Jack Lee.

Lee, himself eighth on City's list of record scorers with 97 goals, was sold to Derby County for £16,000 with Rowley being brought in by boss Norman Bullock on the same day from Fulham. At the time, City fans were fuming, but it turned out to be a good bit of business. After an impressive first season with the Rams, Lee was hit by injuries, while Rowley set about re-writing City's record books. He bagged a late winner at Bury on his debut and went on to end his first season with a 28-goal haul. In the Division Two championship-winning season of 1956-57, Rowley netted 44 times. That haul made him the leading scorer in the country for the second time and remains the most goals scored by a Leicester player during a season. Rowley scored an incredible 16 hat-tricks for City during his eight years with the club and 'The Gunner' predictably marked his final appearance at Filbert Street with a goal for Shrewsbury Town reserves in February, 1963.

Similarly, there wasn't much fanfare when Arthur Chandler arrived at City in June, 1923 from Queens Park Rangers. At the age of 27, many believed he was past his best – and they were all spectacularly wrong. 'Channy' is City's record goalscorer with 273 goals in all competitions that includes six in the record 10-0 pasting of Portsmouth at Filbert Street in October, 1928.

LAST-DAY DRAMAS

Leicester City went to the top of Division Two with victory in their penultimate game of the 1922-23 season – and still ended up missing out on a top-two finish and promotion.

City had been among the challengers at the top for most of the season. They put together what was then a club record nine-game unbeaten run and were seldom out of the top three. Leicester went top of the table with a 2-0 win over Bury at Filbert Street in their penultimate league fixture on April 28th thanks to Tom Smith's double, but two days later they were knocked off the summit following victory for West Ham United. The Foxes still went into the final game of the season at Bury in the second promotion spot, but City headed to Gigg Lane without the injured John Duncan, Mick O'Brien, Billy Thomson and Albert Pynegar. City were beaten 2-0 with future Foxes boss Norman Bullock on target for the Shakers and missed out on promotion on goal average – despite finishing as the division's top scorers.

City scored 65 goals and conceded 44 to leave them with a goal average of 1.477, while West Ham's record was 63–38 for an average of 1.657 and that was enough to take them into the top flight at Leicester's expense. As it turned out, the key result during the season was a shocking 6-0 defeat at home to the Hammers in February.

THE NEXT SEASON

The following season, City inflicted last-day agony on East Midlands rivals Derby County. The Rams needed a 5-0 win in the clash at the Baseball Ground to pip Bury for the second promotion place and they looked on course to do just that when they opened up a 3-0 half-time lead against City. Leicester shipped a fourth goal to leave Derby on the brink of promotion – and then battened down the hatches. Derby couldn't grab a fifth goal and missed out on promotion.

BORO DENIED

Leicester denied Middlesbrough promotion to the top flight on the final day of the 1987-88 season. Boro needed maximum points to go up and were beaten by Peter Weir's opener and a long range Gary McAllister shot as David Pleat's team wrapped up a 2-1 win at Ayresome Park.

MILNE'S SWAP OF HORRORS

Gordon Milne got Leicester City promoted to Division One in his first season at the club, then kept them in the top flight for three seasons. Despite all that, he is probably best remembered by City fans for a transfer deal that has left supporters scratching heads ever since. Jim Melrose had arrived from Partick Thistle in the summer of 1980 for a fee of £250,000 and he top scored with nine goals as Jock Wallace's team battled in vain against the drop.

That haul included the winner at Liverpool and a hat-trick on the last day of the season at Norwich City that condemned the Canaries to the drop alongside City. Melrose added 14 more goals the following season – including two in the epic FA Cup quarter-final victory over Shrewsbury Town – despite starting 11 games on the bench. Wallace left at the end of the season for Motherwell. In came Milne and within a month of taking over he had got rid of crowd favourite Melrose in a swap deal that brought Tommy English to Filbert Street from Coventry City. English had hardly endeared himself to City fans when netting a hat-trick for the Sky Blues in a 4-1 win at Highfield Road in March, 1981 which dealt a massive blow to Leicester's hopes of staying up. His goal scoring touch deserted him when he rejoined former Coventry boss Milne. He found the target only three times in 28 appearances as City were promoted and after misfiring again the following season, English was on his way out. After spells at Rochdale and Colchester United among others, Tommy played for non-league Harwich and Parkeston alongside younger brother Tony and his teenage son.

RAM LEGEND

Roger Davies is a Derby County legend for his goalscoring feats in the side that won the Division One championship in 1974-75. A few junctions down the M1 in Leicester, they would rather forget all about him. Frank McLintock bought Davies from Belgian side Bruges for £250,000 in December, 1977 in the hope he would score the goals that would keep the Foxes in the top division. But he scored just four times in 18 appearances – and one of those looked like an own goal – as City were relegated and he netted twice more the following season before heading off to play in America.

BACK TO THE FUTURE

The club's future was going to be put to the vote and everyone with a Leicester City tattoo held their breath. City were coming out of administration in February, 2003 with the help of a consortium led by chairman Jon Holmes and he decided the best way to make a new start would be to change the club's name back to the one they had ditched almost 84 years earlier!

He suggested the club should be called Leicester Fosse again believing it would make the club unique. Ironically, Fosse had been wound up, taken over and renamed in the summer of 1919 because it owed the United Counties Bank the sum of £3,150 3s 3d. Anyway, the city's tattooists rubbed their hands in anticipation as Holmes' proposed name change was put to the vote. On their way into the Walkers Stadium for the game with Wimbledon on February 22nd, City fans were each handed a card with the letter 'C' and 'F' on it, so they could cast their vote during the half-time interval.

Leicester fans among the crowd of 31,438 voted overwhelmingly against changing the club's name and confirmation at the final whistle of the 4-0 victory came with the announcement: "City will be City forever!" It had all started with a group of former schoolmates in a garden shed. The history books tell us that in the spring of 1884, a group of Old Wyggestonians met in a garden shed just off Fosse Road in Leicester and decided to form a football club. Frank Gardner was among the cofounders. He was elected the club's first secretary and treasurer and years later, claimed to have made the following rather bold declaration at the meeting: "As the Fosse is known throughout the land, so shall the new club be known in the future."

ANOTHER FOSSE

The name wasn't that unique, however. The club's first opponents were Syston Fosse! The sides met at a private playing field just off Fosse Road on November 1st, 1884 after a carpenter had made a set of goalposts reportedly painted amber and black. Leicester wore black jerseys with a diagonal blue sash and long white trousers for the historic fixture and they powered to a 5-0 win. There were two goals apiece for West and Hilton Johnson and Dingley got the other.

ROOSTER!

Kevin Russell owed his cult status at Leicester City to his vital goals – and John Wayne!

As a boy, he was given the nickname 'Rooster' because of his love for the classic Western *Rooster Cogburn* that starred 'The Duke' and it stuck with him throughout his football career.

City fans chanted 'Rooster' and it was suggested Russell got his nickname because he ran around like a headless chicken. 'Rooster' thought there was no such thing as a lost cause and that's just as well because his City career looked like being one. In the months following his £150,000 move from Wrexham in the summer of 1989, Russell spent so much time in hospital that he probably got invited to the staff parties and had to wait until the nerve-jangling climax of the 1990-91 season to show City supporters what he could do. Caretaker boss Gordon Lee handed Russell his chance against Middlesbrough in March, 1991 after a run of four straight defeats had left City in danger of a first-ever drop into the third tier of English football. 'Rooster' responded with a goal in a thrilling 4-3 win.

He added another from the penalty spot in a 2-0 win at Notts County and ended the season with five goals as City survived on the final day of a dramatic campaign. Russell had a similar impact towards the end of the following season when the Foxes were battling away at the other end of the table and his two winning goals in the space of four days fired Brian Little's team to the brink of the Premier League. His late winner against Tranmere Rovers at Filbert Street on April 15th lifted Leicester into the second promotion place and Russell ensured they stayed there with another dramatic goal at promotion rivals Blackburn Rovers three days later.

Russell charged down Rovers goalkeeper Bobby Mimms' clearance and then joyfully ran the ball into the empty net in front of the thousands of travelling Leicester fans. City missed out on a top-two spot and Russell went on to have a crucial role in the play-off semi-finals against Cambridge United. He grabbed the opener in the 1-1 draw at the Abbey Stadium and added another in the 5-0 romp that followed in the second leg and took Leicester back to Wembley after 23 years. Russell drew a blank in the final against Blackburn Rovers at Wembley and to the surprise of most supporters, he left for Stoke City in the summer.

SEVENTH HEAVEN

Leicester have four times put together club-record runs of seven successive wins. They first achieved this feat in the 1907-08 season and the winning run helped Fosse go on to clinch their place in the First Division for the first time. They were eighth before the visit of Blackpool on February 15th, 1908 and the 2-1 win was followed by victories over Derby County (2-1), West Bromwich Albion (3-0), Bradford City (5-1), Hull City (3-2), Glossop (3-2) and Lincoln City (1-0). The promotion charge was halted by a 5-1 reverse at Fulham, but Fosse ended up finishing the season as runners-up behind Bradford.

1924-25

City chalked up seven straight wins again in the 1924-25 season on the way to lifting the Second Division championship. Arthur Chandler's hat-trick powered City to a 5-1 win over Coventry City at Filbert Street on January 24th, 1925 and the next fixture brought a 6-1 demolition of Sheffield Wednesday with 'Channy' on target twice again. That was followed by wins over Clapham Orient (1-0), Barnsley (6-0), Crystal Palace (3-1), Fulham (4-0) and Oldham Athletic (1-0). The last win took City top of the table for the first time that season.

1962-63

City repeated that winning sequence in 1962-63. It all started with a 5-1 win over Leyton Orient and was followed by victories over Arsenal (2-0), Everton (3-1), Nottingham Forest (2-0), Ipswich Town (3-0), Liverpool (2-0) and Blackburn Rovers (2-0), which kept City in the hunt for the Division One championship.

1992-93

City's seven-game winning run in the 1992-93 season vindicated Brian Little's decision to push defender Steve Walsh into the forward line. City were outside the play-off places in the second tier of English football going into the game against Birmingham City in front of the television cameras on February 28th, 1993; they kick-started their challenge with a 2-1 victory. Walsh was on target against the Blues and kept getting his name on the score-sheet as City went on to score three goals in each of their next six games to power into a play-off place. Walsh netted in six of City's seven straight wins.

IS THERE ANYBODY THERE?

Around 2,500 fans turned up to watch Leicester Fosse take on local rivals Loughborough Town in December, 1890 – but they didn't see much! The 1-1 draw was played out in heavy fog and legend has it that Fosse goalkeeper Charlie Walker was left on the pitch at the final whistle and it wasn't until 20 minutes later that his team-mates in the changing room noticed he was missing.

Walker was found still on the pitch and reportedly said he thought the game was still going on and that Fosse were piling on the pressure at the other end of the pitch!

At least the game went ahead. In 1885-86, Fosse set off to take on Leicestershire rivals Old Loughburians and after failing to find the ground, they reportedly spent the afternoon at the races!

ROUGH ON LUFF

Fosse's clashes with Loughborough led to the first reports of football violence in Leicester's history and there were some fiery exchanges on the pitch. In 1893-94, Fosse were accused of "downright ruffianism" by the Leicester press after the FA Cup clash between the sides. There was a 34-minute delay while Luffs defender Jack Kent had a broken leg treated on the pitch. Fosse won the fourth qualifying round match 1-0. The rivalry at Football League level came to an end after the 1899-1900 season as Loughborough finished bottom of Division Two for the second time in three seasons and were not re-elected. Fosse were sorry to see them go having won nine of their ten league matches and drawn the other, but Woolwich Arsenal were glad to see the back of them. The Gunners' record defeat remains the 8-0 mauling they suffered at Loughborough in 1896. Loughborough also had two goals disallowed!

WANDERING INTO TROUBLE

Fosse's early rivals included Burton Wanderers and after a match between the sides in January, 1897, Wanderers full-back Cunningham sank a few post-match pints with his team-mates and then headed off to more pubs in the city to challenge all comers to a fist fight! Someone took him up on his offer and put him in hospital.

GREW DON'T KNOW WHAT YOU'RE DOING

Mark Grew had some big boots to fill – and didn't. Grew was signed by Leicester City boss Gordon Milne in the summer of 1983 as a possible replacement for long-serving goalkeeper Mark Wallington. Wallington and the club were in a contract dispute and that prompted Milne to bring in Grew from West Bromwich Albion for a £60,000 fee. Grew had spent eight years at the Hawthorns, making his debut in a Uefa Cup tie against Galatasaray, and made 33 league appearances for the Baggies. He was handed the goalkeeper's jersey for the opening match of the

1983-84 season against Notts County at Filbert Street and had a horror debut. Martin O'Neill's free kick whistled past him and former Foxes striker Trevor Christie added a hat trick in the Magpies' 4-0 romp.

Four days later, Luton Town were 3-0 winners at Filbert Street and Grew was powerless to prevent further defeats against West Bromwich Albion (0-1), West Ham United (1-3) and Tottenham Hotspur (0-3), which meant he had shipped 14 goals in his first five appearances for the Foxes and probably helped speed up negotiations between Wallington and City. Wallington was back between the posts for the trip to Coventry City and while he couldn't stop a 2-1 defeat at Highfield Road – which made it six straight defeats for the Foxes and a worst-ever start to a league campaign – he kept his place and Grew was relegated to the reserves. After just five games Grew moved on to Ipswich Town and made an unhappy return to Filbert Street at the start of the following season. Television viewers watched him theatrically rip his gloves off and throw them on the ground in front of a joyful Kop after being beaten by Steve Lynex's last-gasp winner. Grew went on to have a successful career at Port Vale and was between the posts for the Valiants when they knocked Tottenham Hotspur out of the FA Cup in the fourth round in 1988.

THE BEST OF THE BEST

Wallington is fourth in the list of average goals per game conceded by City's goalkeepers. He was beaten 607 times in 460 appearances – an average of 1.319 per game – and Peter Shilton tops the list with an average of 1.118 goals conceded per game in his 339 appearances. George Hebden is second with 1.135 goals conceded per game in his 104 games.

SPOT OF BOTHER

Leicester City went into the record books for all the wrong reasons at Anfield in August, 1974 – they conceded the quickest penalty in Football League history with just 19 seconds on the clock.

City kicked off the game at Liverpool, a pass from Malcolm Munro was intercepted by Steve Heighway and he was brought down by Leicester keeper Mark Wallington. Alec Lindsay stepped up to convert the spot-kick and he was only the second Liverpool player to touch the ball in the match. Lindsay went on to add another penalty in a 2-1 win for the Reds. Keith Weller netted City's reply.

AN INNOVATIVE FOX

Fosse goalkeeper Jimmy Thraves had a key role in the introduction of the penalty kick. In February 1891, he was between the posts for Notts County in an FA Cup tie against Stoke City. Thraves was beaten by a shot which defender Jack Hendry punched off the line and Stoke were awarded a free kick. Thraves spread himself right in front of the player taking the kick and smothered his effort. This proved to be crucial as Notts ran out 1-0 winners and the FA later decided to bring in the penalty kick just a year after rejecting the suggestion. Thraves joined Fosse the following year and got off to a stuttering start. He was late for his debut at Mansfield Town after missing his train connection, but went on to be an ever-present for the next four and a half seasons, making 148 consecutive appearances for Fosse.

MILLER MISSED

The penalty kick was introduced for the fixtures played on September 1st, 1891 and on that day, 'Tout' Miller netted from the spot for Burton Wanderers against Great Bridge Unity. Miller went on to join Fosse and missed Leicester's first penalty kick awarded to them at Football League level against Newcastle United at Filbert Street on October 20th, 1894, in a 4-4 draw.

THE FIRST OF MANY

Harry Bailey scored Fosse's first-ever penalty in a friendly against Notts County on September 14th, 1891 and Billy Dorrell grabbed the first in competitive fare in the FA Cup tie against Rushden on October 15th, 1892.

DR. WHO

Leicester City's Youth Academy has produced among others, Gary Lineker, Emile Heskey and Dr. Who! Matt Smith was a prolific goalscorer for City's under-15 and under-16s and was showing plenty of promise according to long-serving Academy manager Jon Rudkin until a serious back injury ended his footballing ambitions. Smith was forced to hang up his boots and a decade later, it was revealed he had landed one of the biggest roles on British television. BBC bosses confirmed in January, 2009 that Smith would be the 11th actor to play Dr. Who having previously had several minor roles.

KNOCKOUT

Heskey was known as 'Bruno' for his resemblance to former world heavyweight boxing champion Frank Bruno and his team-mates, when he played for Leicester Schools, included another who was to bid to conquer the world with his fists. Neil Linford remembers playing alongside Heskey at the heart of what must have been a no-nonsense defence before deciding to concentrate on boxing. He was a top-class amateur with Belgrave Amateur Boxing Club – boxing for England and winning the bronze medal at the European under-19 championships – before turning professional. The biggest night of his career came in Portsmouth in March, 2003 and he planned to walk into battle for his WBU world title fight with Tony Oakey wearing a Leicester City shirt until he was advised against it. At the time, City and Portsmouth were scrapping it out for promotion to the Premier League and it was feared Linford's show of support for Leicester would inflame tensions. Linford had the home favourite on the floor in the 10th round of a gruelling fight before losing a points decision.

NEVER MADE HIS MARK

As a teenager, Mark Walsh was a promising player on Leicester City's books who played alongside Heskey and later became a professional boxer after being released by the Foxes.

DEVOTED

Kevin Concepcion is another Leicester boxer who made no secret of his devotion to the Foxes. Concepcion, the elder brother of another professional boxer, Martin, walked to the ring for his fights in Leicester to the same post-horn gallop tune that greeted City's arrival on the pitch.

THE CUP THAT DIDN'T CHEER

For six years, the FA Cup had all the romance of a slap round the face for Leicester City supporters. Following a run to the fifth round in 1984-85 that was ended by Millwall after wins over Burton Albion and Carlisle United, City didn't win a game in the competition for the next six years. City's reputation in the FA Cup was built in the 1960s when they reached three finals and was left in tatters by third-round defeats against Bristol Rovers, Queens Park Rangers, Oxford United, Manchester City, Barnsley and Millwall. Admittedly, the draw was not kind. They were handed only one home match in that six-year barren spell and were beaten 2-1 by Barnsley in January, 1990. The third round defeat at Millwall the following season was even more devastating. Tony James' goal put David Pleat's team in front and they were just four minutes away from the fourth round when it all fell apart.

Steve Walsh and Paul Ramsey were sent off, Millwall netted twice in the dying minutes and Leicester hearts were broken again. The summer of 1991 brought Brian Little to Filbert Street, and with the new manager came plenty of optimism. He got rid of some players, brought in a few, and gave confidence to those left shell-shocked by the previous season's battle against relegation that was won on the final day thanks to Tony James' goal against Oxford United.

Under Little's leadership, City were soon among the contenders for promotion and the FA Cup draw handed the chance to test themselves against top-flight opposition. They were drawn at home to Crystal Palace and although they had the better of the chances, City couldn't make the breakthrough and the scoreline was blank with the game just seconds away from a replay at Selhurst Park. City had a final chance when they were awarded a free kick.

Gary Mills lifted the ball over to the far post where Richard Smith was lurking unmarked, and rather unexpectedly, to crash his right-foot volley into the roof of the net and spark wild celebrations. Smith was interviewed by Sky Sports as he left the pitch and then headed into the city for a few drinks that he didn't have to pay for. It didn't last, however. The Foxes were drawn at home to Bristol City in the fourth round and in icy conditions, the Robins skated through to the fifth round with livewire winger Junior Bent the inspiration for the visitors and Paul Kitson on target for the Foxes.

CITY AND SIR MATT'S FINISH

Maybe it wasn't Mission Impossible, but it wasn't far off. Leicester City headed to Old Trafford on May 17th, 1969 to face a star-studded Manchester United side, including George Best and Denis Law, needing maximum points to secure their top-flight survival. As if that wasn't enough, United were also determined to give manager Sir Matt Busby a fitting send off as manager in his final game in charge. Three weeks earlier, City had been beaten by Manchester City in the FA Cup Final and after the game, the Foxes were left needing seven points from their remaining five games to stay in Division One for a 13th successive season. Allan Clarke secured victory for City over Tottenham Hotspur and after defeat at Ipswich Town, Ally Brown's debut brace clinched two more priceless points against Sunderland and Graham Cross grabbed City's goal in a 1-1 draw against Everton. All of which meant Frank O'Farrell's team needed to win at Manchester United to stay up. Skipper David Nish gave them the perfect start with a goal in the opening minute. By the fourth minute, City were behind with Best and Law the marksmen for United. The Reds went on to add a third and although Rodney Fern pulled a goal back for Leicester, it wasn't enough to keep them in Division One.

DEVILISH PERFORMANCE

Manchester United were top of Division One when they took on Leicester City at Filbert Street on November 23rd, 1985 and were blown away inside a breathless opening 30 minutes! City handed a debut to loan signing Laurie Cunningham, formerly with United, but it was Gary McAllister and Alan Smith who got the goals that fired the Foxes to a famous win.

McAllister put Gordon Milne's team ahead in the seventh minute – dancing past a couple of challenges before rifling his shot into the corner of the net – and Smith's brace in the space of 15 minutes meant there was no way back for United. Smith doubled the lead and then thumped home number three from what seemed an impossible angle in front of 22,008 disbelieving fans.

City continued to struggle, however, and only secured their safety on the final day of the season when a 2-0 win over Newcastle United at Filbert Street was enough to keep them up at Ipswich Town's expense.

TIME FOR A REST

Gary Mills needed to put his feet up at the end of the 1991-92 campaign. He was an ever-present for Leicester City throughout the season – making a club-record 61 appearances in Division One, the FA Cup, the League Cup, the Zenith Data Systems Cup and the play-offs – as Brian Little made an instant impact at Filbert Street. Unsurprisingly, Mills was named the Supporters' Club's Player of the Season for his efforts. Mills, who collected a European Cup winners' medal while still a teenager at Nottingham Forest, went on to lead out City in the 1993 Division One play-off final against Swindon Town. Twelve months later, he made a memorable contribution to the play-off victory over Derby County – despite not getting on the pitch! He was working as a summariser on local radio and reacted with plenty of enthusiasm when Steve Walsh's second goal hit the back of the net to take Leicester into the Premier League!

SEVEN OF THE BEST

Mark Wallington set a Leicester record by making 331 consecutive appearances between January 4th, 1975 and March 6th, 1982. His run was ended in the unforgettable FA Cup quarter-final against Shrewsbury Town. He was dazed by a collision with Shrews striker Chic Bates and two goals flew past him while he was seeing stars rather than the ball. In the days before substitute goalkeepers, he was replaced by Alan Young and then Steve Lynex and City romped to a 5-2 win that booked a semi-final against Tottenham Hotspur. Young and Lynex both reckoned that keeping a clean sheet meant they had done better than Wallington, but it was Nicky Walker who was between the posts for City at Chelsea three days later and the Foxes were beaten 4-1 at Stamford Bridge.

46ER

The club's first ever-present was Jack Lord. He achieved the feat in Leicester Fosse's debut season in the Midland League and Gary McAllister became the Foxes' first 46-game ever-present in 1988-89. A decade later, Steve Guppy was City's first ever-present in the Premier League. Guppy played all 38 top-flight games as Martin O'Neill's team clinched tenth spot. He also played both FA Cup matches and all eight games in the League Cup campaign that ended with the heartbreak of a last-gasp defeat against Tottenham Hotspur in the final. The following season, Guppy's consistent form on City's left wing earned a call up to England's squad for the friendly against Belgium that ended in a 2-1 win at Sunderland. After that, Guppy was hit by injury and never played for England again.

SAVE IT WITH FLOWERS

Tim Flowers was in the best form of his career – but still couldn't get his own manager to pick him! Flowers had a starring role as Leicester City climbed to the top of the Premier League after the opening eight games of the 2000-2001 season. He kept six clean sheets to help City to the summit of English football for only the fifth time in the club's history and was named the Carling Player of the Month for September. So Flowers had to fancy his chances of an England recall, especially when City boss Peter Taylor was placed in temporary charge of the national team. Taylor had previously been a successful coach of England under-21s and controversially lost his position when Glenn Hoddle took charge. He went on to take a job often referred to as the second most important in the country behind that of Prime Minister following Kevin Keegan's resignation as England manager in October, 2000 after defeat against Germany in a World Cup qualifier. Taylor was appointed caretaker manager for the friendly against Italy in Turin the following month while the Football Association searched for a successor to Keegan and he looked certain to hand Flowers a recall. Flowers had earned the last of his 11 caps for his country two and a half years earlier against Morocco and had impressed since joining City in the summer of 1999 from Blackburn Rovers for a fee that would rise to £1.4 million.

Instead of handing Flowers a recall, Taylor gave the goalkeeper's jersey to David James in Turin. He also appointed David Beckham captain of his country for the first time and Leicester striker Emile Heskey started the game in the forward line. England were beaten 1-0 and although Taylor was set to take charge of the friendly with Spain the following February, Sven-Goran Eriksson took charge before then. Flowers never got the chance to play for England again and injury problems meant that he announced he would be retiring at the end of the 2002-2003 season. Leicester fans were hoping he would mark his last appearance with a goal! Flowers came off the bench in the final match of the season at Wolverhampton Wanderers and when City were awarded a spot kick, the travelling supporters pleaded with Foxes boss Micky Adams to give him the chance to score what would have been the only goal of his career. But the ball was handed to Trevor Benjamin and he netted City's goal in the 1-1 draw.

LEICESTER AND THE LIP

More than three decades after the game, Leicester City fans still breathe a sigh of relief when they watch their side's winning goal hit the back of the net. City's epic FA Cup fourth round tie with Leatherhead in January, 1975 is featured on a BBC DVD of the competition's greatest matches and for the most part, it is X-rated stuff for Foxes supporters and best watched from behind the sofa. At the time, it looked like a great draw for City.

They were paired with a team from the Isthmian League and although Jimmy Bloomfield's team were drawn away, the fixture was switched to Filbert Street. Leatherhead's giant-killing bid would be spearheaded by Chris Kelly and his pre-match boasts that his minnows would dump out City earned him the nickname 'The Leatherhead Lip'. Even his team-mates must have thought he was bonkers. Although City weren't having the best of times in the top division – they were one place off the bottom and without a win in 12 games when the sides met – Leicester could still call upon the talents of Keith Weller and Frank Worthington against the part-timers from Surrey. The previous season, City had reached the semi-finals and bowed out to Liverpool after a replay and had eased to a 3-1 win over Oxford United in the third round to set up the clash with Leatherhead. The BBC cameras and 32,090 fans headed to Filbert Street to see if Kelly could back up his boasts. He almost did.

To the astonishment of the crowd, Leatherhead stunned the Foxes by racing into a 2-0 lead with Kelly netting the second goal and then came the game's turning point. Kelly looked set to bag Leatherhead's third and surely put the game beyond City after rounding goalkeeper Mark Wallington following a swift counter attack, but Malcolm Munro came to Leicester's rescue by sliding across to hack the ball off the line. That escape woke City from their slumbers. Jon Sammels pulled a goal back on 54 minutes before Steve Earle bagged the leveller with 16 minutes remaining. Weller grabbed the third with just ten minutes left to complete City's stunning comeback and ensure they avoided humiliation. Leicester's reward for their great escape against Leatherhead was a fifth-round trip to Arsenal, which was another epic tie. After the sides battled out a goalless draw at Highbury, the replay ended 1-1 at Filbert Street after extra time, and City were beaten in the second replay by an extra-time goal.

THE HIDING OF ALL HIDINGS

The football reporter of the *Leicester Mercury* had had enough. Leicester Fosse were already heading for relegation – and then this…

"Fosse have taken a good many beatings in their time," he wrote in the edition dated April 22nd, 1909, "but they have never participated in such a farcically absurd game as that at Nottingham yesterday. When to the score of 12-0 is added the fact that Bailey made a number of good saves and the Forest goalkeeper was never seriously troubled once during the 90 minutes, it will be seen that the beating was such a one that Fosse have never previously known since they have been a club."

As it turned out, the 12-0 thumping that remains the club's heaviest defeat – and will hopefully remain so – owed much to a few thumping heads among the Fosse players. The scoreline raised a few eyebrows. Only four days earlier, Fosse had beaten FA Cup Finalists Manchester United 3-2 and with Forest also threatened by relegation, the other teams in the survival scrap demanded an investigation into the lopsided scoreline in Nottingham. The investigation came at Leicester's Grand Hotel on May 6th, 1909 and it revealed that the day before the game at Forest, Fosse's players had been to the wedding of former team-mate 'Leggy' Turner in the city and that the celebrations had continued into the early hours. The league accepted this and Fosse escaped punishment. They finished bottom of the table and then had to endure the season's post script from the *Mercury*'s football reporter. He wrote of a season "of falsified predictions, hopes rent in tatters, past feats obscured and fond beliefs shattered, a season of disappointment, depression and almost interminable disaster. Can one wonder that many who follow their fortunes are in despair ? Or can one blame them?

"But let it be the feeling of which a poet wrote: 'Despair is hope just dropped asleep/For better chance of dreaming.'"

Poetry in a *Mercury* football report, eh? Times have changed a bit. Fosse's humbling in Nottingham is still the equal record victory in a top-flight fixture along with West Bromwich Albion's hammering of Darwen in 1892 and is still Forest's biggest-ever league victory. Perhaps Forest had gained extra motivation from the drubbing suffered by neighbours Notts Olympic in an FA Cup qualifying round tie on October 13th, 1894. Fosse handed out a 13-0 hammering with a hat-trick for David Skea and four apiece for 'Tout' Miller and Willie McArthur.

LIGHTS, CAMERAS…

The 1981 film *Escape To Victory* stars among others, Michael Caine, Sylvester Stallone, Pele and a Leicester City player! Caine, Stallone, Pele and Bobby Moore all played the parts of Allied prisoners of war who hatch a plot to escape their German prison camp during the half-time break of an exhibition match against a German team. Russell Osman, who went on to play for City, is against the idea. "But we can win this," he says with all the conviction of a footballer who has never acted before and so the team go out for the second half to battle out a 4-4 draw. At the time the film was made, Osman was with Bobby Robson's Ipswich Town and he went on to make 120 appearances for City. Stallone was in goal for the Allies and made the penalty save that ensured the game finished level – with a bit of help from a pair of Leicester keepers. Gordon Banks helped Stallone prepare for the film and then Paul Cooper stepped in to act as Stallone's stunt double in several scenes and the stumpy keeper must have been pleased with that. There were also roles in the film for Ossie Ardiles and Osman and Cooper's Ipswich team-mates John Wark and Kevin O'Callaghan.

"DO I FEEL LUCKY?"

Leicester City's former Filbert Street home gets a mention in the 1971 classic *Dirty Harry*. Sort of. Clint Eastwood starred as the rule-bending, sharp-shooting cop Harry Callahan and at one point he is speeding through the streets of San Francisco in pursuit of some nasty piece of work or other and orders his partner to: "Throw a left at Filbert." He meant Filbert Street in the American city.

FAVOURITE SON

An Evening With Gary Lineker was a successful play that was turned into a television comedy drama. The story, written by Chris England and Arthur Smith, tells of a couple who head to Majorca to discuss their marriage problems and end up getting wrapped up in England's pursuit of the 1990 World Cup in Italy led by Leicester's favourite footballing son. The television adaptation was shown in 1994 and starred Paul Merton, Clive Owen, Martin Clunes and Caroline Quentin. Lineker himself turned up at the end of the show.

MONEY WELL SPENT

On his arrival at Filbert Street in November, 1936, Jack Bowers became a Leicester City hero sparking an astonishing climb up the Division Two table. Struggling in 17th place when he joined, City ended up being crowned champions!

Bowers had been the top flight's leading scorer three times in four seasons with East Midlands rivals Derby County and that convinced City boss Frank Womack to spend a club record £7,500 to bring him to the club. That was more than double the previous highest outlay of £3,450 which was spent on Len Barry nine years earlier. Bowers wasted little time in repaying City's investment. After marking his debut with a goal in a 3-1 win at Swansea Town, he went on to score in each of his first six games for City, all of which ended in victory to start a sensational climb up the table. His first six games for the Foxes brought 12 goals – including a hat-trick in a 5-1 demolition of Barnsley – and his brace in a 4-1 thumping of Tottenham Hotspur on the final day of the season ensured City finished on top of the table. He finished his first season at City with 33 goals – despite missing the first three months of the campaign! Bowers added another ten goals on City's return to the top flight and when World War II broke out in 1939, he had an incredible record of 219 goals in 282 appearances. He went on to be assistant manager at Derby.

CONSECUTIVE FOR CHANNY

Arthur Chandler holds the record for scoring in the most consecutive games for City. His goal in the 3-0 win at Derby County on December 6th, 1924 marked the start of a run of 'Channy' finding the target in eight successive games. He ended the season with 32 goals in Division Two as City were crowned champions.

ACCURATE ARTHUR

Arthur Rowley scored in seven consecutive games for the Foxes during the 1951-52 season. His goal-den sequence started with City's third goal in a 3-1 win over Coventry City and he added strikes against West Ham United, Sheffield United, Barnsley, Hull City, Blackburn Rovers and Queens Park Rangers.

CRAZY KEEPERS

For a generation of Leicester City fans, Mark Wallington was their team's goalkeeper.

His record-breaking run of 331 consecutive games in goal for City came to an end in an unforgettable clash at Filbert Street. City hosted Shrewsbury Town in the quarter finals of the FA Cup in March, 1982 and were given the perfect start by Larry May's early header. Chic Bates' boot then separated Wallington from his senses and left him seeing stars rather than the ball as it flew past him twice and into City's net to give the Shrews the lead.

Wallington groggily – and reluctantly – left the pitch and his place between the posts was taken by striker Alan Young. He wasn't that badly missed up front thanks to Shrewsbury defender Colin Griffin. He rolled the ball into his own net to level the scores and make Filbert Street erupt.

Young's spell in goal came to an end when he was left dazed after being clattered and winger Steve Lynex pulled on the goalkeeper's jersey to become City's third stopper. Young went back in goal after his head had cleared and Lynex went on to set up Jim Melrose's goal that put the Foxes ahead again at 3-2. That goal knocked the stuffing out of Shrewsbury and further goals from Gary Lineker and Melrose completed a 5-2 win that took City through to a semi-final clash against Tottenham Hotspur. Young and Lynex joked afterwards that they should be in goal for City's next fixture because they had kept out Shrewsbury while Wallington had been beaten twice. Instead, Nicky Walker took the number one jersey shirt for the clash at Chelsea three days later that was lost 4-1.

CAPITAL TRIO

City also used three goalkeepers in a League Cup second round, first leg tie at Crystal Palace in September, 1999. Martin O'Neill's side looked set to take a lead back to Filbert Street for the return leg when an own goal and strikes from Neil Lennon and Gerry Taggart opened up a 3-1 lead at Selhurst Park. But the game turned when goalkeeper Tim Flowers was injured. He had come on to replace Pegguy Arphexad and with all the substitutes used, Theo Zagorakis went between the posts for ten-man City. Palace netted twice in three minutes to draw level, but Zagorakis kept them out in the last 15 minutes.

WEMBLEY WOE

Only Leicester City could stop Tottenham Hotspur securing their place in the record books at Wembley on May 6th, 1961. Seven days earlier, Spurs had clinched the Division One championship and were aiming to become the first team in the 20th century to complete a league and cup double.

City had finished the season sixth and boss Martin Gillies dropped the bombshell of all bombshells when he announced the line up for City's second FA Cup Final. He had decided to drop striker Ken Leek and replaced him with Hugh McIlmoyle. Leek had scored in every round on the way to the final – including a strike in the semi-final win over Sheffield United – and had also starred in City's stunning 3-2 win at White Hart Lane earlier in the season. When quizzed about the decision that stunned City's fans, Gillies said: "There seems to be some kind of mystery in the minds of many people. It is quite absurd to suggest that I made the change for any reason but the interest of the side. I made the change purely and simply because I consider McIlmoyle to be the player in form, and that is all."

That didn't quite add up. Since the semi-final, Leek had scored three goals in four league games and McIlmoyle had been on target four times in seven appearances. To add to the mystery, the pages of the boardroom minute book that covered the pre-cup final meeting have been removed.

Despite the controversy, City actually settled quicker on the big day before disaster struck in front of a crowd of 100,000. In the 18th minute, City full-back Len Chalmers came out of a challenge with Les Allen with a leg injury and in the days before substitutes that meant Leicester had to battle on for the rest of the game with only ten fit players. Chalmers was handed the role of outside-left and Gillies' reshuffle led to Frank McLintock moving into defence and striker Ken Keyworth dropped back. Although they battled on, City were undone by a couple of late goals as their legs tired. Bobby Smith put Spurs ahead in the 69th minute and seven minutes later, a mis-hit from the injured Chalmers sent the Londoners away on the counter-attack and Terry Dyson put the game beyond Leicester with the second goal. That meant Spurs wrapped up the first league and cup double since 1897 and City's squad headed off to Rhodesia and South Africa for a five-match tour.

IT'S NO JOKE

Peter Shilton didn't realise what he had done until he got home and turned on the television. Only then did he understand that his Leicester City team-mates weren't winding him up! Shilton had been between the posts for the City team that stormed to a 5-1 win at Southampton in October, 1967, and was surprised to find himself on the score-sheet alongside Mike Stringfellow (two), Alan Tewley and Jackie Sinclair.

"It was a windy day and I belted the ball down the pitch," remembered the Leicester-born legend. "I saw it drop into the net and presumed somebody got a touch before it went in. I thought the lads were winding me up when they told me it was my goal. I realised they were telling the truth when I got home and turned the television on! A week earlier Pat Jennings had scored against Alex Stepney and everyone seems to remember that. They don't seem to remember my goal!"

Shilton never found the target again in a record-breaking career that started with Sunday morning kickabouts at the club's Belvoir Drive training ground that was next to his family's home and went on to span 1,391 first-class matches and 125 caps for England.

SPOT ON HERBERT

Herbert Bown also found the target for Leicester Fosse, but his goal against Hull City in March, 1917 came from the penalty spot. Bown was also off target in another spot kick attempt.

KEEPER TURNED STRIKER

City's goal scorer in the Midland League clash at Mansfield Town in November, 1940 was the Stags' reserve goalkeeper!

City turned up for the World War Two fixture with only 10 players and Wright took the opportunity to strike a blow in his battle for Mansfield's goalkeeping jersey by twice putting the ball past the player chosen instead of him. Wright lined up at outside right for City and netted both their goals in the game, which was won 4-2 by the Stags.

COTT-GLEE

The pages of Tony Cottee's scrapbook had something missing… From the start of his playing days on the school field, Cottee kept a record of every goal he scored. All those goals – including 116 for boyhood heroes

West Ham United and another 72 for Everton – and not one of them in front of Manchester United's fans at Old Trafford. At the age of 32, Cottee thought his chance had gone and then came the 'prank' phone call that changed all that while he was playing in Malaysia with Selangor.

"My family's business is insurance," he explained, "and we used to insure Steve Walford's house. He was assistant manager at Leicester and my dad rang me up to say there was a chance Martin O'Neill might be interested in signing me. I thought it was a wind up!"

The clubs agreed a £500,000 fee in August, 1997 and Cottee was on his way to Filbert Street to relaunch his career. He had a spell on loan at Birmingham City and on his return, was named in the starting line-up for the clash at Old Trafford on January 31, 1998. It looked like a home banker. United were unbeaten in front of their home fans since the start of the season and had dropped only two points. Earlier in the campaign Juventus had left Manchester empty handed after a 3-2 defeat in a Champions League tie. So it was something of a surprise when Cottee handed City a first-half lead with his first goal at the Theatre of Dreams. Muzzy Izzet put the ball into United's penalty area and Cottee nipped in to lift his shot over goalkeeper Peter Schmeichel and into the net in front of a stunned and silent Stretford End. Emile Heskey almost doubled the lead before the break and City hung on to secure their first win at Old Trafford in 17 attempts. The *Sports Mercury* hit the streets that night with the front-page headline: "Cott-Glee !" and there was more to come from the rejuvenated marksman. He went on to claim the first domestic winner's medal of his career after helping City lift the Worthington Cup with victory over Tranmere Rovers at Wembley in February, 2000. At the end of the season, Cottee and Steve Walsh applied for the manager's positions after the departure of Martin O'Neill in the summer of 2000. Cottee says they both felt the club needed "consistency rather than upheaval" and as it turns out, he was right.

HARD ON HAMILL

When is being a match-winner not enough? When you're Stewart Hamill and Jock Wallace is your manager. Hamill was handed the number 11 shirt for Leicester's home date with Wrexham on September 5th, 1981 and grabbed the only goal. Three days later, he did it again, firing City to a 1-0 win over Barnsley at Filbert Street – and never played for Leicester again!

Hamill wasn't even on the bench for the trip to East Midlands rivals Derby County that came four days after his heroics against the Tykes and he went on to join Scunthorpe United on loan after falling out of favour with Wallace. The Foxes boss had plucked Hamill from Scottish part-timers Pollok, and a job as a Co-op van driver, in September, 1980 to hand him his chance with City. He made eight appearances in the top-flight as Leicester struggled to live up to Wallace's early-season prediction that they would win Division One and then resurfaced the following season for those match-winning heroics before heading for the exit. After leaving Leicester, Hamill then drifted into non-league before marking his return to the Football League with Northampton Town with a goal after just 35 seconds of his debut against Tranmere Rovers, as the Cobblers stormed to the Fourth Division championship. Hamill had a spell at Scarborough and was in the line-up for their first-ever match in the Football League in August, 1987 before returning to Leicestershire to play for Lutterworth Town and Houghton Rangers in the Senior League.

Jack Lee hung around a bit longer than Hamill at Filbert Street. The Sileby-born striker made 163 appearances and netted 97 goals before leaving for Derby County in a £16,000 transfer that caused outrage among Leicester fans. His career as a county cricketer with Leicestershire was rather brief – despite making a dream start to his debut. In July, 1947, he was selected for the County Championship fixture at Glamorgan's Cardiff Arms Park and became one of a select group to take a wicket with their first ball in first-class cricket. He had Glamorgan opening batsman A. H. Dyson caught and also took a catch in the Welsh team's first innings. His bowling figures were 1-13 from four overs. Lee didn't get the chance to bowl in the second innings – and never played for Leicestershire again.

BACK AT WEMBLEY

Third time lucky? Not a bit of it. Believe it or not, but there was a time when Leicester City went into the FA Cup Final against Manchester United as red-hot favourites. It was May, 1963 and City were fancied to lift the trophy at the third attempt having failed in previous finals in 1949 and 1961, against Wolverhampton Wanderers and Tottenham Hotspur respectively. Seven days earlier, they had finished the Division One season in fourth place after being top of the table with just five games remaining, while United had narrowly escaped relegation from the top flight.

City had been unbeaten in their two meetings in the league. They met twice in as many days and after drawing 2-2 at Old Trafford, Leicester were 4-3 winners the following day at Filbert Street with Ken Keyworth the hat-trick hero and Denis Law bagging a treble in reply. It proved to be Leicester's last win of a season that promised so much and ended with Matt Gillies' team missing out on any silverware. They ended the league season with four defeats away from home and perhaps still suffering from the disappointment of missing out on what would have been the club's first ever championship, City's stars then went on to freeze on the big day at Wembley in front of a 100,000 crowd. City's line-up included three new internationals – Gordon Banks, Frank McLintock and David Gibson – while Colin Appleton had represented the Football League and Graham Cross had recently gained his first cap for England under-23s. Yet it was United's Pat Crerand who proved to be the match-winner with a masterly display in midfield, setting up the opening goal for Denis Law in the 29th minute. Law took Crerand's pass, spun and rifled his shot past Banks. City struggled to get into the game and it took until the 37th minute before Cross had their first shot of note.

United felt they should have been further ahead at the break and went on to double their lead 12 minutes after the interval after an uncharacteristic mistake by Banks. He mishandled a shot which gifted David Herd the chance to pounce and net the rebound. City were back in it with just nine minutes left. Keyworth's diving header handed them a lifeline, but another mistake by Banks allowed Herd to net his second goal, and United's third, to put the game beyond the Foxes and leave them still waiting to win at Wembley.

A NEW ERA

At the end of the 2001-2002 season, Leicester City left behind their rather ramshackle Filbert Street home and headed over the road to the brand spanking new Walkers Stadium. Still, there were plenty of tears after the last game at Filbert Street which saw a 2-1 win over Tottenham Hotspur. It always is hard to leave home. Unfortunately, City started life in their new home outside the top flight following relegation from the Premier League, but the club did line up a prestigious pre-season friendly against Spanish giants Athletic Bilbao on August 4th, 2002 – the first game played at the Walkers Stadium. Jordan Stewart went into the history books as Leicester's first goalscorer in their new home. He struck to cancel out Tiko's opener and ensure a 1-1 draw for Micky Adams' team in front of a crowd of around 24,000 fans. Six days later, City played their first league fixture at the ground and were 2-0 winners over Watford in front of a crowd of 31,022. Brian Deane headed home the opener in the first half and later added the second. The Walkers Stadium proved to be a happy home for City in their first season there. Their promotion back to the Premier League was confirmed by a 2-0 win over Adams' former club Brighton & Hove Albion, the team's 16th win in front of their own fans – a new record for the most home wins during a season and City's haul of 92 points at the end of the campaign was another club record.

FRIENDLY INTERNATIONAL

The Walkers Stadium has also staged international football. In June, 2003, England took on Serbia and Montenegro in a friendly watched by 30,900 fans – and City goalkeeper Ian Walker! Walker was on the bench for the clash and – despite the pleas of the locals – that's where he stayed throughout a 2-1 win. Joe Cole was England's hero. He lashed home the match-winning free kick with just eight minutes left after Steve Gerrard's opener had been cancelled out on the stroke of half time. Four months later, Brazil and Jamaica met at the Walkers Stadium in another prestigious friendly that was settled by a stunning strike. Brazil full-back Roberto Carlos launched a 15th minute free kick that swerved into the corner of the net.

MADRID MISERY

Thirty-six years after their first misadventure, Leicester City headed back into European competition and history repeated itself. City

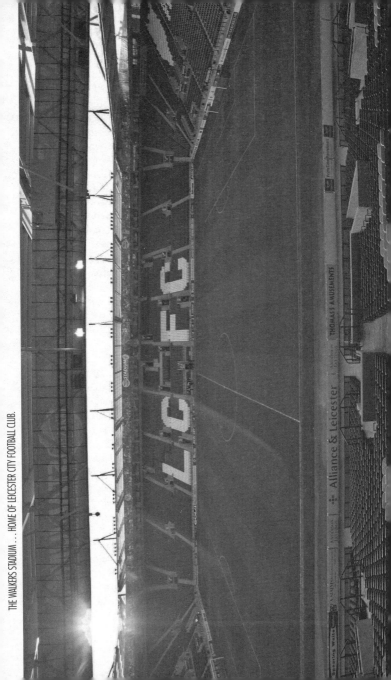

THE WALKERS STADIUM . . . HOME OF LEICESTER CITY FOOTBALL CLUB.

lifting the Coca-Cola Cup after victory over Middlesbrough in the final replay at Hillsborough in April, 1997 ensured their qualification for the following season's Uefa Cup. Their League Cup success in 1964 hadn't been rewarded with the chance to take on the continent's cream and City's only previous involvement in European competition had been in the 1961-62 season when Tottenham Hotspur winning the Football League and FA Cup double meant Leicester represented England in the European Cup Winners' Cup. Their interest back then was ended by Atletico Madrid after some controversial refereeing decisions in the second leg – and more than three decades on, Martin O'Neill's team suffered a similar fate. City's supporters headed over to Spain in their thousands for the first leg – and many were soon wishing they hadn't. The conditions on many of the coaches were described as insufferable, but the mood of the travelling fans was lifted just 11 minutes after the action got underway at the Vicente Calderon Stadium. To the astonishment of most of the 35,000 crowd, Ian Marshall put City ahead when he hooked home from close range and Leicester set about hanging onto their lead.

The introduction of winger Jose Mari turned the game Madrid's way as he helped unlock City's defence, but it was a familiar face who levelled the scores. City's effective shackling of Brazilian Juninho had been one of the keys to their Coca-Cola Cup success five months earlier and he got his revenge for new club Atletico. He grabbed the equaliser with the help of a deflection off Steve Walsh and Christian Vieri's late penalty ensured Atletico held a 2-1 advantage going into the second leg at Filbert Street two weeks later. Roared on by a crowd of 20,776, City launched wave after wave of attacks from the opening whistle and felt they should have been awarded four penalties with Muzzy Izzet having three appeals rejected after he was sent crashing. The sending off of Antonio Lopez gave City a boost, but the advantage was controversially wiped out when Leicester playmaker Garry Parker was also dismissed. Parker was handed his marching orders for taking a free kick too quickly and with him went City's hopes of overturning the deficit. Leicester were deflated by the sending off and Madrid went on to snatch victory with late goals from Juninho and Kiko that took them to a 3-1 win on aggregate.

LEICESTER LEGENDS

Leicester City's top ten all-time appearance makers

Graham Cross 599
Sep Smith 586
Adam Black 556
Hugh Adcock 460
Mark Wallington 460
Willie Frame 459
Steve Walsh 449
Mal Griffiths 420
Arthur Chandler 419
John Sjoberg 413

Graham Cross holds the record for making the most appearances for Leicester City. In a first-team career with his home-town club spanning more than 14 years, Cross played for City 599 times and would surely have made 600 appearances if he hadn't been so good at cricket.

He was a sporting all rounder and his decision to help Leicestershire win cricket's County Championship for the first time in their history in 1975 rather than report back for pre-season training with City spelled the beginning of the end of his time at Filbert Street.

His first visits to City's home had come as a seven-year-old when his heroes were Arthur Rowley and Johnny Morris. Cross went on to make his debut as a 17-year-old and marked his first appearance with a goal against Birmingham City. He went on to spend his 18th birthday playing at the heart of Leicester's defence in front of 50,000 fans as City took on Atletico Madrid in the second leg of their second-round tie in the European Cup Winners' Cup. City were beaten 2-0, but Cross emerged with plenty of credit. He also played in two FA Cup Finals and two League Cup Finals during Leicester's golden era in the 1960s and says the best memory of his career with the Foxes came at Blackpool's Bloomfield Road ground on April 8th, 1963. Ken Keyworth's goal secured a point for City from a 1-1 draw and that was enough to take Leicester to the top of Division One.

Adam Black actually betters Cross's tally of 495 + 3 appearances for City in the Football League with 528 appearances. Sep Smith had the lengthiest first-team career with Leicester. Smith made his debut on August 31st, 1929 and then 19 years, 249 days later he made his final appearance on May 7th, 1949.

HE'S NO SAINT

There are only two Matt Elliotts. There was the towering, commanding presence at the back for Leicester City and then, er, there was the towering, commanding presence up front. Martin O'Neill needed all his persuasive powers to bring Elliott to Filbert Street in January, 1997. Having previously convinced Neil Lennon not to go to Coventry City – can't have been that difficult – O'Neill then secured Elliott's signature in a £1.6 million deal when he looked to be heading for Southampton. Elliott missed out on City's Coca-Cola Cup triumph because he was cup tied and instead took on the role of television summariser in the matches with Middlesbrough. He had a crucial role to play in the Premier League and it was Elliott's goal in the penultimate game against Sheffield Wednesday that finally made City safe and helped them to a ninth-place finish. City's impressive start to the following campaign – they were third after nine games – led to Elliott's call-up for Scotland.

Elliott, born in Wandsworth and with an accent to match, qualified through a Scottish grandmother and was on the bench throughout his adopted country's World Cup campaign in France in the summer of 1998 after helping the Foxes finish tenth. That was followed by another tenth-place finish and an appearance in the Worthington Cup Final in the 1998-99 season. Elliott's comfort on the ball, aerial prowess and powerful shooting meant O'Neill would often push him into City's forward line and it was from this position that he powered the Foxes through to their third League Cup Final in four years. He headed home the only goal of the two-legged semi-final against Aston Villa and then bagged both in the final victory over Tranmere Rovers at Wembley in February, 2000, which earned him the man-of-the-match award and led to more chances up front – particularly after Stan Collymore suffered a broken leg in a 3-0 defeat at Derby County at the start of April. City went on to finish eighth and Elliott had his first taste of European football at club level the following season in the Uefa Cup.

After O'Neill's departure, Elliott went on to lead out City in their first game at the Walkers Stadium on the opening day of the 2002-2003 season and went on to skipper Micky Adams' team to promotion back to the top flight. City were relegated the following campaign, however, and Elliott retired in January, 2005 having been troubled by a knee injury for two seasons. He made 271 appearances for City.

JOCK'S SOS

Who better to help rescue Leicester City from relegation than a player once rated the best in the world? Manager Jock Wallace took City to the Division Two championship in 1979-80 and predicted they would add the Division One crown the following season after seeing Andy Peake's wonder goal and a Martin Henderson strike sink Liverpool at Filbert Street. The title challenge didn't materialise, however, and as well as suffering FA Cup humiliation at Exeter City in a fourth round replay, Leicester also found themselves battling against the drop from the top flight.

They were one place off the foot of the table in February, 1981 with 11 games of the season left when Wallace announced his intention to bring Dutch star Johan Cruyff to the club. Although 33 years old and beyond his peak, Cruyff had once been rated as the best player in the world.

He was named Player of the Tournament after the 1974 World Cup where he was part of the Netherlands side that thrilled the world with their 'Total Football' on their way to the final where they were beaten 2-1 by West Germany. He was named European Footballer of the Year in 1971, 1973 and 1974. Cruyff retired from international football in 1978 having scored an impressive 33 goals in 48 appearances for the Dutch and was without a club in February, 1981 after a spell in the North American Soccer League. The news that Leicester were bidding to sign him dominated back pages. Wallace reportedly put together a deal offering Cruyff between £4,000 and £5,000 per game and was convinced the payment would be recouped by an increase in attendances at Filbert Street. The *Leicester Mercury* dated February 24th, 1981 revealed that Wallace had agreed terms with Cruyff and Foxes fans held their breath.

But Wallace missed out on what would have been one of the biggest signings in the club's history. Two days after he predicted Cruyff was on his way to Leicester in the *Mercury*, the Dutchman's agent informed Wallace that he was on his way to Spanish club Levante after a lucrative deal had been agreed. Levante reportedly offered Cruyff 50 per cent of gate receipts for their matches and that offer was too good to turn down. City battled on without him and although they claimed Arsenal's scalp at Filbert Street and then finished the season with back-to-back wins over Birmingham City and Norwich City, it wasn't enough to prevent an instant return to Division Two for Wallace's team.

RECORD BREAKERS

Leicester City's 2008-2009 season went into the record books for the wrong reasons and the right reasons. They kicked off their first campaign outside the top two divisions in English football and went on to set a new club record unbeaten run.

City's last-gasp 2-1 win over Bristol Rovers at the Walkers Stadium on November 1st, 2008 kick-started a 23-match unbeaten run in League One that powered the Foxes into a 12-point lead at the top and set them on their way to promotion back to the Championship at the first attempt.

The previous longest unbeaten league run had been 19 games and Nigel Pearson's team set a new record with a 1-0 win at Bristol Rovers in February, 2009 that made it 20 matches unbeaten. It took a Max Gradel goal seven minutes into injury time to extend the run seven days later and that was followed by a draw against Stockport County and a 4-0 trouncing of Cheltenham Town before the run was ended by a 2-0 defeat at Tranmere Rovers on March 11th, 2009.

THE OTHER SIDE OF THE TRACKS

Nigel Pearson, the manager at the helm when City put together their longest unbeaten run in the league, was an unlikely Leicester hero. For a start, he was born in Nottingham and then he tried to stop the Foxes claiming their first piece of silverware for 36 years. Pearson was at the heart of Middlesbrough's defence in the Coca-Cola Cup Final in

1997 which was won by Steve Claridge's extra-time strike in the replay at Hillsborough. On top of all that, Pearson then condemned City to their first season outside the top two divisions. He was in charge of the Southampton team that survived on the last day of the 2007-2008 season at City's expense. Fortunately, he made amends for all that.

THE ONLY WAY IS UP

Leicester's previous longest unbeaten run in the league had started on February 6th, 1971 with a goalless draw at Hull City. They had stretched the without-a-loss sequence to 17 games by the end of a season that finished with City lifting the Division Two championship. The Foxes then started the 1971-72 top-flight campaign with a draw at Huddersfield Town and a win over Nottingham Forest before a 2-0 defeat at Derby County.

A GAME OF CARDS

A bit of advice. If you have a late-night game of cards with Dennis Wise, make sure you sleep with one eye open afterwards. Sadly, Wise's spell with Leicester City is remembered more for the impact he had on team-mate Callum Davidson's cheekbone than the impact he had on the pitch. Wise was a legend with Chelsea where he won the FA Cup twice, along with the League Cup and the European Cup Winners' Cup and it cost City £1.6 million to prise him away from Stamford Bridge in the summer of 2001. He made his debut for Peter Taylor's team in a 5-0 opening-day defeat at home to Bolton Wanderers that wasn't exactly the perfect way to start City's final season at Filbert Street. City struggled, Taylor was sacked and Wise's continued poor form attracted plenty of criticism from the stands. At the end of the campaign, Leicester were relegated from the Premier League after six seasons in the top flight and part of the preparations for the promotion bid under Micky Adams' leadership was a pre-season tour of Finland.

There the squad trained, played friendlies and had a game of cards that got a bit out of hand. Wise was sent home for inflicting a double fracture of Davidson's cheekbone after dishing out some retribution while the Scottish international lay asleep. City then announced the decision to sack Wise with two years of his contract still left to run. The club were ordered by the Football League to reinstate him and after that decision was overturned, Wise announced his intention to sue the cash-strapped club for lost earnings totalling £2.3 million. It came to nothing and Wise ended up joining Millwall with his return to City for a fixture in December, 2002 much anticipated by Foxes fans.

It was another former City player who put the Lions in front with just 14 seconds on the clock. Steve Claridge shrugged apologetically when his name was read out over the Tannoy. To be fair, he simply couldn't miss the target. There was a happy ending, however, and not just for the groundsman who got a Christmas bonus when picking up the coins that had been hurled at Wise throughout. City ran out 4-1 winners with James Scowcroft finding the target twice for Adams' team. The other goals came from Matt Elliott and Paul Dickov. Wise then went on to add to his villain status at Leicester by becoming something of a hero at Midlands rivals Coventry City.

HEADING FOR THE TOP

On January 1st, 1979, Leicester City supporters headed for the Filbert Street exits talking about the teenage striker who looked destined for the top. A few probably talked about Gary Lineker as well. City boss Jock Wallace handed debuts to David Buchanan, Bobby Smith and Lineker in the 2-0 win over Oldham Athletic in Division Two and it was Buchanan who made the headlines.

He was on target at the age of just 16 years and 192 days to become the club's youngest goalscorer and Smith added the other, while 18-year-old Lineker drew a blank, was dropped and had to wait three months for a wet night at Notts County to open his account for City. That scrambled effort marked the start of one of the most prolific goalscoring careers of the modern era. Never booked or sent off in 15 years as a professional, Lineker, the son of a Leicester marker stall trader, is the second highest goalscorer for England and a national hero.

He first came to prominence with a 17-goal haul in Division Two in 1981-82 and the following season he became the first City player since Arthur Rowley in 1956-57 to score 25 league goals in a season as Gordon Milne's team put together a 15-match unbeaten run that helped Leicester pip Fulham for the third promotion spot. Lineker continued to flourish in the top flight and his 22-goal haul in 1983-84 earned a first England cap as a second-half substitute against Scotland at Hampden Park. The goals kept coming and after 24 the following season, Lineker was sold to Division One champions Everton in June, 1985 for £800,000. In total, he netted 103 times in 216 appearances for City and after 40 more goals in his only season with the Toffeemen, the former City of Leicester School pupil came to global prominence at the 1986 World Cup in Mexico where his six strikes earned him the Golden Boot as the tournament's highest scorer and a £2.75 million move to Barcelona.

Lineker went on to score 48 times for England in 80 appearances and would have levelled Sir Bobby Charlton's record had he netted with a penalty against Brazil at Wembley in May, 1992. His final appearance for England came in that summer's European championships in Sweden after manager Graham Taylor replaced him with former City strike partner Alan Smith in a clash with the hosts. Lineker ended his playing career with former Leicester boss Gordon Milne at Nagoya Grampus Eight in Japan.

INTO EUROPE

As it turned out, Leicester City still had reason to celebrate following defeat in the 1961 FA Cup Final. Tottenham Hotspur's 2-0 win completed a league and cup double and that meant City were England's representatives in the following season's European Cup Winners' Cup. The first-round draw sent them to Irish Cup holders Glenavon and in front of a crowd of 10,000 at Windsor Park, City fell behind to Sid Weathercup's opener before easing to a 4-1 win through goals from Jimmy Walsh (2), Colin Appleton and Ken Keyworth. City went on to wrap up a 7-2 aggregate win with a 3-1 victory in the second leg at Filbert Street. Gordon Wills, Ken Keyworth and Hugh McIlmoyle were the marksmen and 10,445 were there to see it.

The second round pitted City against Spanish giants Atletico Madrid and Matt Gillies' team had home advantage in the first leg. Their preparations were far from ideal with goalkeeper Gordon Banks arriving at the ground only 40 minutes before kick-off having been on the bench for England against Portugal at Wembley earlier that day. Ken Keyworth gave the majority of the 25,527 crowd reason to cheer by putting City ahead having earlier had an effort controversially ruled out, which proved to be crucial. City looked set to take the lead with them to Spain, but Mendoza popped up with a late leveller for Madrid.

Gillies sprang a surprise before the second leg when his team sheet revealed that Graham Cross would spend his 18th birthday at the heart of City's defence in front of more than 50,000 fans. Cross, a goalscorer on his debut on the final day of the previous season, was making only his fourth start for City and while he impressed with a mature display, it was the performance of the officials that dominated Gillies' post-match thoughts. He was enraged by the decision to award Madrid two penalties. Banks kept out the first, but was beaten by the second and the home side went on to complete a 2-0 win and a 3-1 aggregate victory.

VIVA

City were set to go back to Spain at the end of the season to take on the Spanish national team as they prepared for the World Cup in Chile, but the FA blocked Gillies' team from playing matches in Santander and Bilbao.

WHICH GOAL?

Aston Villa defender Chris Nicholl grabbed the headlines after grabbing all the goals in the game with Leicester City at Filbert Street on March 20th, 1976. Nothing too unusual in that. Except that the game finished 2-2! Nicholl scored two goals at both ends just seven days after Stuart Boam's own goal had gifted City a 1-0 win at Middlesbrough in Division One. A decade earlier, Graham Cross grabbed all the goals in City's 2-1 win over Nottingham Forest at Filbert Street. He made amends for putting the visitors ahead by bagging both goals for the Foxes. Leicester legend Steve Walsh holds the club record for scoring the most own goals. He scored against City seven times with his spectacular long-range effort in the 2-1 defeat at

Arsenal in the Premier League on December 26th, 1997 taking him past Dai Jones and Graham Cross's tally of six own goals each.

TO BE FRANK

Walsh's team-mate Frank Sinclair also forgot which way he was kicking a few times. At the start of the 1999-2000 season, he scored an own goal in the opening-day 2-1 defeat at Arsenal, followed seven days later with another in the 2-2 draw against former club Chelsea at Filbert Street. Perhaps his most spectacular own goal came in the Premier League game at Middlesbrough in March, 2002. His back pass from 40 yards left Ian Walker stranded and was the only goal of the game as the Foxes headed for relegation. On the occasion Sinclair was supposed to put the ball past the Leicester goalkeeper, he blew it. Sinclair returned to his former club with Lincoln City for a Johnstone's Paint Trophy tie in September 2008 and after two hours of goalless and tedious football, the game went into a penalty shoot-out. As the drama reached its climax, Sinclair was handed the job of keeping the visitors in the tie and walloped his spot-kick high, wide and pretty ugly, much to the delight of City's fans behind the goal.

DOUBLE TROUBLE

City defenders Stan Milburn and Jack Froggatt shared an own goal in the 3-1 defeat at Chelsea in December, 1954. They managed to somehow simultaneously kick the ball and send it into the Foxes' net.

FLYING STARTS

Best not miss the kick-off when Matty Fryatt is in the starting line-up. He holds the record for scoring the quickest-ever goal for both Leicester City and previous club Walsall. Fryatt went into City's record books on April 15th, 2006 with a goal after just nine seconds of the home game with Preston North End in the Championship. He was also on target for Walsall after nine seconds of their clash with AFC Bournemouth on March 12th, 2005. His early goals didn't set either City or Walsall on their way to victory. Both teams were eventually beaten 2-1.

Fryatt joined City from the Saddlers in January, 2006 to boost the battle against the drop from the Championship and his six goals helped fire the Foxes to safety. Twelve months later, he was almost on his way out of Filbert Street. But, in the whirlwind of signings that followed Martin Allen's appointment as City boss in the summer of 2007, perhaps the best bit of business was the transfer that didn't happen. Allen decided striker Fryatt was worth more than the £1 million Wolverhampton Wanderers bid for him and while a few months later he wasn't even worth a place in the first team, there was to be a happy ending to Fryatt's story. He scored only three goals throughout a wretched 2007-2008 season that ended with Leicester being relegated to the third tier of English football for the first time in their history. The following campaign Fryatt became City's first striker since Derek Dougan 42 years earlier to net 20 goals before Christmas.

He reached the milestone with back-to-back hat-tricks at the Walkers Stadium against Dagenham & Redbridge in the FA Cup second round, and Southend United in League One.

TEN TEN TEN

Before Fryatt's whirlwind goal, the record for City's fastest strike was shared by three players with a time of ten seconds. On March 28th, 1953 Tom Dryburgh got City off to the perfect start against Swansea City at Filbert Street and Leicester went on to win 2-1. Eight months later, Derek Hines' goal after ten seconds set City on their way to a 9-2 demolition of visitors Lincoln City. Hines added four more goals in the Division Two clash. City went on to win the title and a crucial win as their next Division Two championship-winning season was clinched with the help of a quick strike. Ian McNeill rifled home after ten seconds of the clash at title rivals Nottingham Forest on March 30th, 1957 to set up a crucial 2-1 victory.

MATT THE GENT

Who says nice guys always finish last? A criticism aimed at Matt Gillies during his decade in charge of Leicester City was that he was "too gentlemanly" for the cut and thrust of professional football. But that didn't prevent him becoming one of the most successful managers in the club's history. Gillies kept the team in the top flight for ten years, took them to Wembley for the FA Cup Finals in 1961 and 1963 and twice led them to League Cup Finals. He first came to Leicester as a player.

After spending a decade with Bolton Wanderers and captaining them in the First Division, Gillies joined City for £9,500 in January, 1952 and boss Norman Bullock's investment proved to be wise. Gillies had a key role at the heart of City's defence in the side that won the Second Division championship in 1953-54 – missing only three of the 42 games – but lost his place during the following season's struggle. Gillies made a total of 111 appearances for City and was also known for his tactical insights. He had already turned down the offer of a coaching job in Italy when he became coach at Filbert Street in April, 1956. Following manager David Halliday's departure in November 1958, with City struggling in the top flight, Gillies took on the caretaker manager's job and City's instant revival under his leadership led to him landing the job permanently two months later.

His transfer dealings were shrewd – the £7,000 he paid Chesterfield for goalkeeper Gordon Banks was considered a gamble at the time – and Gillies became the first Leicester manager to guide the team to silverware when he led them to the League Cup in 1963-64 with victory over Stoke City. The following season, Leicester were beaten in the final by Chelsea. Gillies suffered with a stress-related illness while he was at Filbert Street, but his departure in November, 1968 was prompted by the sacking of his long-serving coach Bert Johnson. Gillies was quick to praise Johnson's input during his decade in charge and followed him out of Filbert Street after he was dismissed. Although the spell in charge at Nottingham Forest that followed was unsuccessful, Gillies did bring Martin O'Neill to the City Ground and the switch to Leicester's East Midlands rivals did nothing to harm his place in the affections of Foxes supporters. His death in December, 1998 led to a perfectly-observed minute's silence before the Premier League game against Blackburn Rovers.

POST-HORN GALLOP

Leicester City started a new era at the Walkers Stadium on August 10th, 2002 and many fans were fuming before the game had even kicked off!

City marked the switch from Filbert Street to their plush new home with a game against Watford in the second tier of English football in front of a crowd of 31,022.

Many among them were stunned when City ran onto the pitch for the historic fixture and there was no post-horn gallop played over the public address. That probably sparked more post-match conversations than the stadium or the 2-0 win over the Hornets secured by Micky Adams' team by a brace from striker Brian Deane. The tune had accompanied Leicester teams onto the pitch since 1941 and was dispensed with following the move from Filbert Street. Not for long it wasn't.

City fans rang the club and *Leicester Mercury* offices demanding the tune was brought back and Foxes officials obliged and the post-horn gallop was soon being blasted out again. It didn't do the team any harm. They went on to win 16 home games in their first season at the Walkers Stadium – setting a new club record on their way to promotion to the Premier League.

The post-horn gallop was chosen as a reference to Leicestershire's hunting tradition and dates back to the 19th century when it was used as a coachman's tune to signal mail was arriving. According to the internet, the tune is also a traditional finale at formal dinner functions.

LIVE VERSION

The club went a step further at the start of the 2003-2004 season. They brought in Henry Shipley to play the post-horn gallop while wearing riding boots and jodhpurs. Henry had previously played in brass bands that performed at Filbert Street in the 1930s and 1940s and enthusiastically blew his bugle to accompany the Leicester team's arrival for home games for two seasons.

The club decided after that to change their pre-match entertainment and that meant the end for Henry and his bugle! He was told he would no longer be able to play the post-horn gallop when City ran out and instead was offered a slot 15 minutes before kick-off. Henry declined because he felt the ground would be half full when he played the song and that it wouldn't be worth his effort.

SEEING RED

Leicester Fosse showed plenty of fighting spirit at Bolton Wanderers in March, 1905. Bob Pollock and Ike Evenson showed too much of it and both were dismissed for fisticuffs. Incredibly, Fosse hung onto the lead given to them by Arthur Collins' strike to win the Division Two clash.

There have been three other occasions when two Leicester players have been sent off in the same game. Kevin MacDonald and Alan Young ran the bath water early during the 2-1 loss at Brighton & Hove Albion in April, 1981 that confirmed relegation from the First Division for Jock Wallace's team and equally dispiriting was the double dismissal at Millwall in the FA Cup a decade later. City headed to The Den without a win in the competition for five years and Paul Ramsey and Steve Walsh were sent off as the Lions cancelled out Tony James' opener for Leicester with goals in the 86th and 89th minutes. David Lowe and Brian Carey were dismissed in the 2-1 defeat at Wimbledon in the Premier League in September, 1994. Lowe had earlier grabbed the Foxes' goal. City had a club record eight players dismissed during the 1994-95 season, which ended in relegation.

THE FIRST

Willie Freebairn was the first Leicester player to be sent off. The Fosse full back was dismissed in the Division Two clash at Lincoln City in April, 1897 for abusing a linesman. Freebairn had earlier scored in the 2-1 defeat.

FILBERT FIRST

David Walker went into the record books as the first player to be dismissed at Filbert Street. He was sent off against Clapham Orient in April, 1911, but his goal still proved to be the winner in a 2-1 victory for Fosse.

FILBERT FLOP

Ade Akinbiyi was a £5 million flop for Leicester City and his career at Burnley got off to the worst possible start following his £600,000 transfer from Stoke City. Akinbiyi was sent off just two minutes after stepping off the bench to make his Clarets debut against Sunderland in March, 2005. He was given his marching orders for trying to elbow and head-butt George McCartney.

TAKING A DIP

Steve Lynex is remembered for his place in Leicester City's 1980s strikeforce alongside Gary Lineker and Alan Smith – and his breaststroke! Lynex, an exciting winger who bagged 60 goals in 240 games, got the chance to show off his swimming skills at a soaking Filbert Street on October 15th, 1983. City and Southampton splashed around in front of the *Match of the Day* cameras in atrocious conditions until the officials abandoned the game after 22 minutes. Perhaps the moment that helped decide the officials to end the farce came when Lynex slid face first through a puddle and simulated a breaststroke! Harder to accept for Leicester fans must have been the decision to abandon the home game against Newcastle United in February, 1936 with City leading 2-1 and just 10 minutes left on the clock.

City's path to the FA Cup Final in 1961 was delayed by the weather. Their fourth-round tie against Bristol City at Filbert Street was abandoned at half-time because of a waterlogged pitch with the score goalless and three days later, City were 5-1 winners. Thirty-one years later, the sides met at the fourth-round stage of the FA Cup at Filbert Street after the game was given the go ahead despite severe frost and the Robins coped better to run out 2-1 winners in front of the *Match of the Day* cameras.

In total, six games were abandoned at Filbert Street and the club's first game to fall victim to the weather came at Darwen on December 30th, 1894. The game was abandoned after just two minutes when the goal posts were blown down by a gale. They ended up playing a friendly that Fosse lost 6-0 before the sides met again 16 days later – and the conditions weren't much better!

The referee allowed one set of goal posts to be moved onto the adjacent cricket pitch and Darwen's players took measures to combat the severe elements. They strapped their boots in swathes of felt to cope with the mud, puddles and sand that covered much of the pitch and they dealt with the conditions better than Fosse. Darwen led 7-0 at half-time and went on to win the game 8-2. City fared better when their clash at Reading in the 2002-2003 season had to be played again. The original fixture on January 1st, 2003 was washed out at half-time with the scoreline blank and Leicester went on to win the rearranged fixture 3-1 on their way to promotion.

WHAT A START!

Jimmy Bloomfield was appointed Leicester City manager in the summer of 1971 – and saw his new team lift a trophy after his first game in charge. Arsenal winning the league and FA Cup double in 1970-71 meant the following season's Charity Shield curtain raiser was between newly-promoted Leicester and Liverpool, who had lost to the Gunners in the FA Cup Final.

The meeting at Filbert Street was settled by Steve Whitworth's strike – his only goal in 400 appearances for City in all competitions! Bloomfield had got the job after the departure of Frank O'Farrell to Manchester United and set about putting together one of the most exciting teams in City's history. His first signing was Jon Sammels from Arsenal after the player admitted he was "95 per cent" certain to join Ipswich Town. Sammels remembers Bloomfield's footballing philosophy.

"Jimmy didn't fill your head with tactics and what he wanted you to do," he said. "He put together a skilful team and didn't complicate things. He used to say: 'I've brought you here because you are good players, so go out there and play.' We played football the right way."

Bloomfield made his intentions clear with the further additions of Keith Weller, Alan Birchenall and after a 12th place finish in his first season in charge, he brought in Frank Worthington after a move to Liverpool fell through because of a failed medical. City finished 16th in 1972-73 and the following season, they were in contention for honours. They were fourth in January after a 5-0 thumping of Ipswich Town, with Worthington the hat-trick hero, and the following month, their 4-0 win at Luton Town in the fifth round of the FA Cup led to comparisons with world champions Brazil! Leicester went on to finish ninth and lose to Liverpool in an FA Cup semi-final replay. They finished seventh in 1975-76 and the following season, City ended up 11th despite a disappointing spell of only one win from their final ten games that included a 5-0 humbling at home to West Bromwich Albion. Less than a week after the end of the season, Bloomfield resigned and one of the club's most exciting eras was over.

Bloomfield still had a role to play in Leicester's future. He was in charge of the Leyton Orient side beaten by Larry May's header on the final day of the 1979-80 season which resulted in Jock Wallace's City being promoted to the top flight as Division Two champions. Jimmy died in April, 1983.

OUT OF LUCK

Patrick Kisnorbo's scrapbook is unlikely to have many cuttings from the 2007-08 season. He was wrongfully dismissed twice during a wretched campaign that ended with his Leicester City team being relegated outside the top two divisions of English football for the first time in their history.

City were outside the drop zone when they headed to Ipswich Town in December, 2007 and with six minutes to go before the break at Portman Road, the scores were level at 1-1. Iain Hume cancelled out Pablo Counago's opener for the home side and the Town striker was then involved in the game's turning point. He went down under a challenge from Kisnorbo that won the ball outside the penalty area. Despite that, referee Phil Joslin took the advice of his linesman and decided to dismiss Kisnorbo and award Ipswich a penalty. Alan Lee converted the spot kick, Ipswich added a third in the second half through Jonathan Waters and then the Football Association decided to rescind Kisnorbo's red card.

Unfortunately, it happened all over again later in the same season. There were just ten minutes gone in struggling City's clash at Sheffield United in April, 2008 when Billy Sharp took a tumble and Kisnorbo was red carded by referee Mike Pike after he had pointed to the penalty spot. James Beattie stepped up to convert the penalty and went on to complete a hat-trick in just seven minutes that left the Foxes deep in trouble at the bottom of the Championship. City boss Ian Holloway was fuming afterwards. "Sort your life out, Billy Sharp," he said. "You

FILBERT FOX JOINS IN THE FUN WITH IAIN HUME AFTER A CITY GOAL.

ain't on my Christmas list, you little turkey. That was the biggest blunder I've seen in a long time."

At least Holloway was handed a boost a few days later with the news that Kisnorbo's red card had been wiped off and that meant he would be eligible for the final four games of the season. Kisnorbo didn't finish the campaign, though. City needed to beat Sheffield Wednesday at the Walkers Stadium in their penultimate game of the season to secure their survival and all was going well when Iain Hume gave the Foxes an early lead. But they suffered a massive setback on 20 minutes when Kisnorbo was stretchered off with a broken leg and the Owls went on to win 3-1 and beat the drop. Eight days later, City's proud record of never having played outside the top two divisions in English football was ended following a goalless draw at Stoke City.

GETTING SHIRTY

Leicester City's away strip in the 1983-84 season was so unlucky that they only recorded a single victory wearing it – and still ended up losing the game! City's ghastly green and gold strip did not bring Gordon Milne's team much luck. They were 2-0 winners at Chelsea in the second leg of their League Cup second round tie in October, which left the scores level on aggregate following City's 2-0 defeat at Filbert Street. Leicester then lost the game on penalties and never won another game in the strip before it was ditched at the end of the season.

BATTLE OF THE FOSSES

Leicester Fosse kicked off their first-ever match against Syston Fosse on November 1st, 1884 wearing black jerseys with a diagonal blue sash and white trousers. Although the kit lasted only two seasons, the shirt made a comeback in City's 2002-2003 Premier League campaign as part of the change strip for Micky Adams' top-flight team.

CAMBRIDGE COLOURS?

Fosse wore a new strip for the start of the 1886-87 season. They wore chocolate and blue halved shirts and white shorts. There was another change four seasons later with Fosse kicking off their debut season in the Midland League wearing white shirts and dark shorts. That kit lasted until the 1899-1900 campaign when Leicester took to the pitch in Cambridge blue shirts and dark blue shorts. The club switched kits again for the 1901-02 season. Fosse wore dark blue shirts with light blue collars and sleeves and white shorts which was worn for two seasons. In the summer of 1903, the club decided to change to a strip of blue shirts and white shorts that were established as Leicester's colours.

NOT ALRIGHT

City have ditched their traditional blue-and-white strip on a couple of occasions. They wore an all-white kit in 1972-73 that proved to be unpopular and lasted only that season. Then there was the all-blue strip worn in 1966-67 and again in 1992-93. On the latter occasion, it lasted for four seasons.

A TROPHY AT LAST

Eighty years of hurt for Leicester City supporters ended at Filbert Street on April 22nd, 1964. Previously beaten in three FA Cup Finals, City lifted their first major trophy since being formed in 1884 with skipper Colin Appleton getting his muddy mitts on the League Cup after a 4-3 aggregate win against Stoke City.

Football League secretary Alan Hardaker could hardly contain his excitement. He enthused: "This is the cure for most of soccer's ills… more games like this."

Admittedly, the League Cup was his idea, but there was no denying the drama served up by City on their way to the trophy. Wins over Aldershot, Tranmere Rovers, Gillingham and Norwich City clinched a two-legged semi-final against West Ham United. City were 4-3 winners at Filbert Street and goals from Frank McLintock and Bobby Roberts wrapped up a 6-3 aggregate win and took Matt Gillies' team through to the final to face Stoke. Leicester travelled to the Potteries for the first leg and it took Gordon Banks' acrobatics and the woodwork to keep out Stoke in the first half. Banks could do nothing to prevent Keith Bebbington lashing Stoke into a 62nd minute lead and it took a superb piece of opportunism from David Gibson to ensure City went into the second leg level. A clearance was deflected into his path and Gibson lifted a perfectly-weighted chip over the goalkeeper's head and into the net from 20 yards to leave Stoke stunned.

Leicester were soon ahead in the second leg played seven days later. Mike Stringfellow latched onto John Sjoberg's clearance to thump home the sixth-minute opener and after Stoke levelled two minutes after the restart, City stepped up a gear. Gibson's near-post header put them back in front and Howard Riley's left-foot shot made it 3-1. Stoke's second goal in injury time came too late to deny City. The following season, City got through to the League Cup Final again and this time they met Chelsea in the two-legged final after wins over Peterborough United, Grimsby Town, Crystal Palace, Coventry City and Plymouth Argyle. The quarter-final win at the Sky Blues was by an 8-1 scoreline and must have been unpleasant viewing for Ken Keyworth. He completed a move from Leicester to Coventry on the day of the match!

The first leg of the final ended in a 3-2 defeat at Chelsea with Colin Appleton and Jimmy Goodfellow on target before a goalless second leg at Filbert Street meant the trophy headed to London.

GETTING HOT AND SWEATY

For Leicester City fans, the last home game of the season means sunshine, tension and The Birch looking shattered!

For every season since 1979-80, Alan Birchenall MBE has set off on a charity run around the Filbert Street and Walkers Stadium pitches, dragging some of football's biggest names along with him including David Beckham and Graeme Souness. All have joined him for a lap or two before kick-off and helped raise more than £700,000 for 70 charities across Leicestershire. The Birch was awarded the MBE for his charity work in 2004 and five years later, he was named an Honorary Freeman of the City of Leicester.

He admits to being "quite embarrassed" by the accolades that have followed since he hung up his boots. Birchenall, of course, was part of one of the most exciting teams in Leicester's history. Along with Jon Sammels and Keith Weller, he was among the first signings made by Jimmy Bloomfield after he became City manager in the summer of 1971. He was an energetic striker and midfielder and the left foot that he dubbed 'The Claw' memorably sent the ball crashing into the Leeds United net at Filbert Street in October, 1973.

He found the target 14 times in 183 appearances for the Foxes and went on to rejoin the club in a public relations role he was clearly well suited to. There was nothing in the job description about running around the pitch before the last game of the season, though. That came about after a member of the Supporters' Club approached The Birch during the 1979-80 season and asked for help raising funds for charity.

"I didn't fancy abseiling or chucking myself out of a plane," said Birchenall, "but I had only just finished playing, so I was still fairly fit and came up with the idea of running round the pitch for 90 minutes before the last home game."

He has been doing it ever since, but admitted: "I've lost count of the times I've said this is the last run." The most laps Birchenall has completed is 63 and he has never ran less than 50 – and he usually does it in sweltering conditions. "It's usually the hottest day of the year when I do the run," he laughed. "I can only remember one year when it wasn't baking hot." The Birch remembers with fondness the year when £75,000 was raised to help former team-mate Keith Weller receive cancer treatment that prolonged his life.

POOR STARTS

Leicester City's future and past combined to ensure the Foxes had the worst possible start to the 1983-84 season in Division One. Martin O'Neill belted home the opener for Notts County at Filbert Street and former City striker Trevor Christie fired home a hat-trick to secure a 4-0 win for the Magpies. City went on to survive the drop despite losing their first six games, while O'Neill made amends for that goal by becoming one of the best managers in Leicester's history.

TROTTER THRASHING

Leicester had a similarly disastrous start to the 2001-2002 campaign – their last at Filbert Street. Bolton Wanderers left with the points after a 5-0 thrashing and City went on to be relegated from the Premier League.

TAKE THAT

Legend Steve Walsh won't remember the opening day of the 1987-88 season with any fondness after breaking the jaw of Shrewsbury Town striker David Geddis and being handed an 11-match suspension.

RAMPANT ROWLEY

The opening day of the 1950-51 season marked the start of a glorious Leicester career. Arthur Rowley made his debut, scoring the winning goal in a 3-2 win at Bury. He went on to score 265 goals for the Foxes.

EXPLOSIVE

Leicester City were quick out of the blocks at the start of the 1971-72 season. Already boosted by winning the Charity Shield with victory over Liverpool at Filbert Street, they started the Division One campaign under Jimmy Bloomfield by scoring the fastest goal of the opening day's fixtures. Ally Brown was on target with just 45 seconds on the clock at Huddersfield Town and City went on to claim a point from a 1-1 draw.

TOFFEE TIME

Gary Lineker's debut for Division One champions Everton on the opening day of the 1985-86 season was ruined by Mark Bright's brace that fired Leicester City to a 3-1 win at Filbert Street. Bobby Smith also netted for Leicester.

M69 DERBY

The footballing cities of Leicester and Coventry are separated by the M69 and much more besides. They simply don't get on and as with any rivalry, there's plenty of history to it. The sides were locked in a battle against the drop from the top division in 1968-69 and the manner in which their derby battle at Highfield Road was decided didn't do an awful lot for relations between the rivals.

Leicester had booked their place in their fourth FA Cup Final of the decade with a 1-0 win over holders West Bromwich Albion at Hillsborough and then three days later they headed to Coventry for an April Fool's Day relegation clash that wiped the smile off City's faces after the euphoria of the win over the Baggies. The game was goalless with just seven minutes to go. Foxes substitute Brian Greenhalgh was brought down as he charged towards goal and the referee awarded a penalty. The ball was placed on the spot and then the referee consulted his linesman and much to Leicester's astonishment, changed his mind about the penalty award and instead decided to give the Sky Blues a free kick. City were deflated and while they protested and rued their luck, the Sky Blues made the most of their good fortune to race up the other end where Neil Martin was on target within seconds of the Foxes having placed the ball on the penalty spot!

Leicester went on to be relegated and lose the FA Cup Final, while the Sky Blues survived by the skin of their teeth. Fast forward almost two decades to the final day of the 2007-2008 season and City and Coventry were fighting it out to avoid the drop into the third tier of English football.

On an afternoon of unbelievable tension, the survival scrap went down to the closing minutes and with relegation rivals Southampton winning against Sheffield United and the Sky Blues losing at Charlton Athletic, City knew grabbing a winning goal at Stoke City would save themselves and send Coventry down. But the goal didn't come and it was the Foxes who suffered the drop. City can take satisfaction, however, from recording one of the biggest wins in their history at Highfield Road.

Ken Keyworth made the switch from City to the Sky Blues on December 1st, 1964 and then saw his former employers beat his new club 8-1 in a League Cup fifth round tie with two goals apiece for Mike Stringfellow, Billy Hodgson and Richie Norman.

BUST UPS

Rewind to December, 1954 and we find Leicester City struggling at the bottom of Division One. The club's directors asked manager Norman Bullock to resign at the end of the season, but events in a Whitley Bay hotel brought forward his departure from Filbert Street. After a 2-0 defeat at Newcastle United in February, 1955, Bullock was involved in an incident that led to him resigning immediately while inside-forward Johnny Morris was handed a 14-day suspension. The pair had a history of conflict with Morris being briefly transfer-listed during pre-season after requesting to train with former club Derby County. Morris ended up staying with City, but his conflict with Bullock clearly had not been resolved. Unsurprisingly, City suffered the drop at the end of the season, but their points total of 37 was the highest achieved by a relegated team since 1937-38.

VOTED OUT

The biggest match in the opening weeks of the 1999-2000 season was City boss Martin O'Neill against Barrie Pierpoint, the club's Chief Executive Officer. The simmering conflict between the football and commercial sides of the club reached boiling point in September, 2000 when club chairman John Elsom and Sir Rodney Walker, chairman of the plc, both resigned. That led to an EGM being called and Elsom and Walker had the backing of both O'Neill and Leicester legend Gary Lineker and their challenge came from the so-called 'Gang of Four'. They became a gang of one following the resignation of Roy Parker, Gilbert Kinch and Philip Smith at the EGM and Pierpoint was voted off the board. Elsom put together a new board of directors that included former chairman Martin George and ex-director Bill Shooter.

HYPERBOLE

A bust up between City chairman Milan Mandaric and boss Martin Allen led to the latter leaving the club in August, 2007 after just 96 days and four games in charge. Quite why they fell out will probably never be known, but another book could be filled with all the rumours that went around Leicester after Allen left the club. The incident most widely

MARTIN ALLEN AND MILAN MANDARIC . . . BEFORE IT ALL WENT WRONG.

believed to have signalled the end for Allen was his apparent reluctance to sign former Chelsea striker Jimmy Floyd Hasselbaink after Mandaric had lined up the transfer.

FILBERT FOX

Filbert Fox, Leicester City's fluffy, feisty mascot, made his debut in 1992-93 and has been conducting the crowd's chants and mischief-making ever since. He has brought along girlfriend Vicky Vixen to matches and Cousin Dennis has also made a few appearances. When he isn't watching his favourite football team or doing good deeds in the local community, Filbert is winning awards. In February, 2009, Filbert scooped the *Leicester Mercury's* Mascot of the Year award for the third successive year – and he earned his trophy the hard way. He took on rivals including Charlie Fox from Leicestershire County Cricket Club and Leicester Tiger from, er, Leicester Tigers at 10-pin bowling, shooting basketball hoops and then a test of football dribbling skills. At the end of it all, Filbert was the winner.

OTHER MASCOTS

Unlike some other mascots, Filbert Fox has managed to steer clear of major controversy. In January, 2006, Wolverhampton Wanderers' mascot Wolfie famously came to blows with one of Bristol City's Three Little Pigs at Ashton Gate and Swansea City's Cyril The Swan has faced a charge of bringing the game into disrepute. Cyril was hauled in front of a three-man commission at the Welsh FA in April, 1999 after the referee at Swansea's FA Cup clash with Millwall took exception to his celebration of a goal by his team. He was banished from the touchline, the club were fined £1,000 and a nine-foot tall swan left the hearing to face the press! Cyril is well loved in Swansea and Hartlepool United's mascot H'Angus The Monkey is so popular in his home town that he was voted mayor in 2002!

H'Angus takes his name from a famous incident in the town's history. In the early 19th century, British forces battled to stop Napoleon and his French forces invading and when a monkey was washed ashore from a shipwreck off the Hartlepool coast, he was hanged by locals fearing he was a French spy. The good folk of Hartlepool have since been known as 'monkey hangers'.

H'Angus The Monkey made his debut at Hartlepool's Victoria Ground in 1999 and became so popular that the club backed H'Angus – or rather Stuart Drummond who wore the costume – to run for mayor. "Vote H'Angus" implored the campaign posters: "He gives a monkey's." Incredibly, he won and made headlines all over the world.

TEARS UNDER THE TOWERS

At the age of 21, David Nish became the youngest player to captain a team in the FA Cup Final when he led out Leicester City at Wembley in April, 1969. Ninety minutes or so later, he became the fourth Foxes skipper to suffer defeat in the domestic game's biggest final. City's preparations for their fourth final – and third of the decade following defeats against Tottenham Hotspur and Manchester United in 1961 and 1963 respectively – were far from ideal.

They were scrapping for survival at the bottom of Division One after only one win in their previous eight games and boss Frank O'Farrell had injury worries. John Sjoberg was ruled out through injury, while Len Glover played despite not appearing to be fully fit and David Gibson had to pass a late fitness test. It took some determined defending to keep out Manchester City in the opening minutes and then Allan Clarke helped get the Foxes into the game. His rasping shot was superbly saved by Harry Dowd and from the resulting corner, Rodney Fern's cross flashed across goal and Manchester City breathed a sigh of relief. They did so again moments later when Peter Rodrigues shot just wide from five yards out. The cross proved to be costly. In the 23rd minute, Mike Summerbee cut the ball back from the right-hand byeline and Neil Young's sweetly-struck shot flew past Peter Shilton's fingertips and into the top corner.

The *Sports Mercury* reported that night: "It was rather ironic that Leicester should withstand the early sustained pressure and then go behind just as they seemed to be getting a grip on the game." Inspired by Clarke, City had their chances after the break and Andy Lochhead missed the best of them. His miscued shot sent the ball over the crossbar when he was well placed just a few yards from goal. That was City's best chance of an equaliser and although beaten at the final whistle, at least they had the satisfaction of having the game's outstanding player in their side.

Clarke, who cost City a then British transfer record fee of £150,000 when he joined from Fulham the previous summer and had netted the only goal in the semi-final win over holders West Bromwich Albion, was named man of the match.

The result sent an eight-year-old Gary Lineker sobbing all the way back home to Leicester and that night's *Sports Mercury* reported: "Manchester City were clearly the more polished, assured side and deserved their victory."

THE START OF AN ERA

On the morning of December 17th, 1995, Martin O'Neill was Norwich City's manager and Mike Walker was the red-hot favourite to take over at Filbert Street after Mark McGhee walked out to join Wolverhampton Wanderers. All that changed on a dramatic day.

After a bust-up with Norwich chairman Robert Chase, O'Neill quit as Norwich boss just hours before the Canaries took on City at Filbert Street. Walker was at the game in the role of television analyst and there was plenty to analyse as City overturned a 2-0 deficit to snatch a 3-2 win with Emile Heskey grabbing the winner. Five days later, O'Neill was named Leicester's new manager and one of the most successful eras in the club's history began. Not that there was much indication of the thrills to follow in the opening weeks of O'Neill's reign. City were dumped out of the FA Cup by Manchester City after a 5-0 thumping at Maine Road, crowd favourite Julian Joachim was sold to Aston Villa and after achieving his first win as Leicester boss at the tenth attempt at McGhee's Wolves, O'Neill came under fire from some fans after a defeat at home to Sheffield United on March 30th.

Three days later, City kick-started their promotion charge with a win at

Charlton Athletic courtesy of Steve Claridge's first goal for the Foxes and four days later, Iwan Roberts was the goal hero at Crystal Palace. City went on to end the season with four straight wins to secure a play-off spot. Garry Parker got the only goal of the two-legged semi-final against Stoke City and the Foxes were back in the Premier League after Claridge's last-gasp goal beat Crystal Palace in the play-off final at Wembley. Tipped for relegation the following season by the bookies, City, boosted by the arrival of Matt Elliott from Oxford United, finished ninth and claimed their first trophy for 33 years. After City and Middlesbrough battled out a 1-1 draw in the Coca-Cola Cup Final at Wembley, Leicester won the replay at Hillsborough thanks to Claridge's extra-time strike.

Under O'Neill's management, Leicester went on to secure four successive top-10 finishes in the Premier League and reach two more cup finals. They were beaten by Tottenham Hotspur in the 1999 Worthington Cup Final and the following season, were back at Wembley to lift the trophy after a 2-1 win over Tranmere Rovers. O'Neill left at the end of the 1999-2000 season to join Celtic and soon ended Rangers' domination of Scottish football.

PROMOTED ON THE BEACH

The battle for promotion in 1982-83 went to the final day of the season and beyond. Leicester City's players had their feet up and were enjoying the sunshine on their end-of-season break when they finally discovered what league they would be playing in the following campaign.
Back then, there were three automatic promotion places up for grabs and City looked set to miss out.

They showed some promise with a 6-0 demolition of Carlisle United secured by hat-tricks from Gary Lineker and Steve Lynex, and Gordon Milne's team went on to kick-start their charge in front of the lowest home league gate at Filbert Street since the war. There were just 6,155 fans there in February, 1983 to watch Gary Lineker's double fire City to a 3-2 win over Shrewsbury Town that took them up to fourth. Four days later, City followed with a 5-0 thumping of promotion rivals Wolverhampton Wanderers that included a thunderbolt from Alan Smith and two goals from Steve Lynex. City kept the run going. Lineker became the first Leicester player since 1957 to net 25 times in a season with a brace in the 3-2 win over Rotherham United that stretched the unbeaten run to ten games and set up a crucial trip to third-placed Fulham. Ian Wilson was City's hero with a shot that bobbled into the net to secure three priceless points at Craven Cottage. Leicester went on to snatch third spot from the Cottagers with just two games remaining in the season. They tightened their grip on the final promotion place with a 2-1 win at Oldham Athletic. Robbie Jones marked his debut with the goal that put City on their way to victory and left them the favourites to go up on the final day of the season. City took on relegation-threatened Burnley in front of a bumper crowd of 29,453 at Filbert Street knowing that victory would secure promotion. They could only draw 0-0, but defeat for Fulham at Derby County meant that would be enough for the Foxes. City celebrated at the final whistle and then waited for their promotion to be confirmed after a controversial ending at the Baseball Ground.

The referee had ended the game 75 seconds early after a pitch invasion by Rams fans and Fulham demanded that the game be replayed. The Football League decided to hold an enquiry and ruled that the result should stand, so City were promoted after ending the season with a 15-match unbeaten run.

THE TELETEXT STRIKER

If Leicester City's players and supporters needed any added confidence before the FA Cup quarter-final against Wycombe Wanderers in March, 2001, they only had to look at Teletext.

There they would find Wycombe boss Lawrie Sanchez appealing for unattached strikers to contact him after an injury crisis robbed him of eight forwards. Roy Essandoh's agent read the story – which had been initially posted on the club's website – contacted Sanchez and so started the beginning of the end for Leicester boss Peter Taylor. City were red-hot favourites going into the contest. They had beaten York City, Aston Villa and Bristol City to reach the quarter-finals and seven days before the visit of Wycombe, they beat Liverpool 2-0 at Filbert Street to lift them up to fourth in the Premier League. Wycombe were struggling a couple of divisions below, but frustrated City in the first half and it took a flying save from Leicester goalkeeper Simon Royce to keep out Steve Brown's long-range shot. Five minutes after the interval, Brown helped put Wycombe ahead. His free kick picked out Paul McCarthy to head home and City suffered another blow on the hour when Robbie Savage had to limp off. But they were level on 67 minutes when Muzzy Izzet converted Darren Eadie's cross and most of a 21,969 crowd breathed a sigh of relief. There was more drama to come and when Wycombe had a 78th minute penalty appeal turned down after Brown's cross was blocked by Stefan Oakes, boss Sanchez was so incensed that his protests led to him being sent from the dugout. Sanchez, no stranger to FA Cup romance having scored Wimbledon's winner against Liverpool in the 1988 final, watched the rest of the match on a television and saw the game come to an astonishing climax.

Deep into injury time, Wycombe had a corner that was nodded across goal to Essandoh and he jumped unmarked to steer his header past a flat-footed Royce and into the top corner in front of a stunned Kop. Brown was rather churlishly sent off for his celebrations and seconds later, City were out. It was a shocking upset and worse was to follow for City as their season fell apart.

They suffered a club record eight successive defeats in the Premier League. The run was ended by a 4-2 hammering of Tottenham Hotspur at Filbert Street before the season ended with a 3-1 defeat at Leeds United which meant City finished the season 13th having been top in October.

DOWN TO THE WIRE

The battle for First Division survival in 1985-86 went all the way to the last game of the season. Not that anybody seemed to care.

Unthinkable though it may seem now, there were just 13,171 fans at Filbert Street on May 3rd, 1986 to see the relegation scrap reach its conclusion. Gordon Milne's Leicester City needed to beat Newcastle United and hope relegation rivals Ipswich Town slipped up at Sheffield Wednesday to stay in Division One. City went into the game having taken just one point from their previous four games – their last win had come at Ipswich – but Ali Mauchlen walloped home the opener from long range and Ian Banks netted the second from the penalty spot to secure a 2-0 win. That was enough. Ipswich were beaten at Hillsborough resulting in their relegation alongside West Bromwich Albion and Birmingham City.

SAME OLD SAME OLD

Twelve months later, City had a new manager and a similar problem. Bryan Hamilton was at the helm with Milne moved into a general manager's role and the partnership got off to a good start with City climbing as high as ninth in October with a 3-1 win over Nottingham Forest at Filbert Street. Then it all went wrong. Seven days after that, City were beaten 2-0 at Charlton Athletic and their slide down the table was underway. Although there were back-to-back four-goal maulings of Queens Park Rangers and Manchester City in the space of four days at Filbert Street, Leicester's away form was appalling. They suffered 17 straight defeats on their travels, so it was far from ideal that their Division One fate would be decided on the final day of the season at Oxford United. City ended their wretched away form with a goalless draw at the Manor Ground, but it wasn't enough to keep them up.

SORRY BORO

The following season, City were involved in more final-day drama – and this time it was at the other end of the table. Unfortunately, it was Middlesbrough rather than Leicester going for promotion and goals from Peter Weir and Gary McAllister secured a 2-1 win for David Pleat's team at Ayresome Park and denied the Teessiders a First Division berth.

ENGLAND EXPECTS

Back in 1974, England came calling for Leicester City's stars. City team-mates Peter Shilton, Keith Weller and Frank Worthington all lined up for their country in friendlies against Northern Ireland, Scotland and Argentina. They had starred in a City side that boss Jimmy Bloomfield steered to ninth place in Division One in 1973-74, and through to the semi-finals of the FA Cup before bowing out to Liverpool after a replay. Weller got the only goal in the 1-0 win over Northern Ireland with a rare header and Worthington was on target in the 2-2 draw with Argentina. England were beaten 2-0 at Hampden Park. David Nish, who had spent six years with City before leaving for East Midlands rivals Derby County, was also in the teams that faced Northern Ireland and Scotland.

THE BIGGEST STAGE

Gordon Banks, of course, was between the posts for England when they lifted the World Cup in 1966 and two decades later, Leicester players were in the thick of the action again. Gary Lineker and Peter Shilton, both born in Leicester and former City players, had key roles at opposite ends of the pitch in Mexico in 1986. Lineker's six goals earned him the Golden Boot for being the competition's top scorer, while Shilton was in goal throughout the tournament and beaten by Maradona's infamous 'Hand of God' goal in the quarter-final defeat against Argentina. Lineker and Shilton also represented their country at the next World Cup in Italy four years later when England reached the semi-finals before bowing out to Germany on penalties.

HIGHS & LOWS

Horace Bailey became the first Leicester player to represent England when Fosse's goalkeeper lined up for his country in the 7-1 thrashing of Wales in Wrexham in March, 1908. Bailey was described by the *Leicester Mercury*'s football reporter as having "an eye like a hawk and cat-like agility" and he helped the United Kingdom XI strike gold at the 1908 Olympics. He made five appearances for England – shipping just three goals and watching 35 fly in at the other end – and if they were the highlights of his career, the lowlight came when he was in goal for Fosse in the record 12-0 defeat against Nottingham Forest in April, 1909.

BOYS FROM BRAZIL

According to *The Sunday Times*, it was just like watching Brazil – on a muddy pitch in Luton. At the final whistle of the FA Cup fifth round tie at Kenilworth Road on February 16th, 1974, the reporter breathlessly told his copy taker he hadn't seen anything like it since the last time he watched Brazil. Believe it or not, he was talking about Leicester City.

After Frank O'Farrell left for Manchester United, Jimmy Bloomfield took on the Leicester manager's job in the summer of 1971 and won a trophy in his first game in charge! City lifted the FA Charity Shield with a 1-0 win over Liverpool in a game that pitted the champions of the top two divisions together and Bloomfield went on to put together a team that thrilled the nation.

Despite that, before the FA Cup tie at Luton, there were those who fancied the Hatters' chances of pulling off an upset. Although seventh in the top tier, City hadn't scored in their previous two games and took on a home team on their way to promotion to Division One.

Conditions were not expected to suit flair players such as Frank Worthington and Keith Weller and the key figure for the Hatters was Leicester legend Rodney Fern. He had made the move from Filbert Street in the summer of 1972 after 187 appearances and 40 goals for City and when he sent an early header flashing just over the bar, the home crowd sensed an upset. Steve Whitworth also hacked a shot off City's goal-line before the Foxes took charge. The opening goal came when Alan Birchenall sent Dennis Rofe racing away down the left flank and Steve Earle got to his cross before the defender to steer his shot into the corner of the net. Weller was inches away from doubling the lead after another slick attack and City hit top gear after the break. The lead was doubled when Len Glover twisted and turned his way past the mesmerised full-back and then sent over a cross that Earle headed into the top corner.

Weller carved out number three. He won the ball in midfield, accelerated away and crossed for Frank Worthington to head home. Weller then completed the scoring with the best goal of the lot. He danced his way through the mud and several challenges before smacking an unstoppable left-foot shot into the top corner of the net. It was later voted Goal of the Season by ITV viewers.

DE-PLEATED

David Pleat arrived at Filbert Street with a reputation. Actually, he arrived with two reputations, but we won't mention the other one. Leicester City were in desperate trouble in December, 1987. They sacked manager Bryan Hamilton after sliding into the relegation places in Division Two and were in the middle of a run of seven games without scoring a goal. The manager's job probably wasn't the most attractive in football and Pleat was highly rated, but circumstances brought Pleat and City together.

After getting Luton Town into the top division and then keeping them there, he masterminded a revival at Tottenham Hotspur – leading them to the FA Cup Final in 1987 and turning them into championship challengers – before a tabloid smear campaign led to his departure from White Hart Lane. As with most relationships, all went swimmingly with Pleat and City before the cracks started to appear. His first signing was classy left-winger Peter Weir from Aberdeen and City set about playing their way out of trouble. They put together a run of five wins in six games which made them the form team in the division and a final day win at Middlesbrough denied the Teessiders promotion and ensured Leicester went into the following campaign tipped as title favourites along with Chelsea. All did not go according to plan in the summer, however, with Russell Osman leaving for Southampton. Weir followed him out of Filbert Street a few months later because his family couldn't settle in Leicester.

Still, the signings of Jimmy Quinn, the division's top scorer the previous season, and goalkeeper Martin Hodge, among others, meant there was plenty of optimism going into the 1988-89 campaign. It proved to be misplaced. They got as high as ninth in December, but the play-off challenge faded and City ended the season with a run of five games without a win to finish the season 15th. The summer brought more changes with Mike Newell leaving for Everton in a £600,000 deal which also brought Wayne Clarke to Filbert Street. Other signings included Tommy Wright. Yet still City struggled and it took the arrivals of loan signings Kevin Campbell and Paul Moran from Arsenal and Tottenham Hotspur to ensure they lifted themselves to 13th at the end of the season. The 1990-91 campaign started with a 3-2 win over Bristol Rovers and was followed by seven successive defeats. Pleat could only temporarily halt the slide and he was sacked following a 3-1 defeat at home to Blackburn Rovers in January.

BIG SIGNINGS

Mark Draper became Leicester City's first £1 million signing when he joined from East Midlands rivals Notts County in July, 1994. He cost £1.25 million and while his classy midfield promptings weren't enough to keep City in the Premier League, his value soared. Twelve months after joining, Draper left to rejoin former boss Brian Little at Aston Villa in a £3.25 million deal.

Matt Elliott also proved to be a wise investment. He was brought to Filbert Street in a £1.6 million move from Oxford United in January, 1997 and went on to be a key figure in Martin O'Neill's side that clinched four successive top-ten Premier League finishes.

BIG FRANK

The signing of Frank Sinclair in August, 1998 set a new record for City's biggest transfer. He came to the club in a £2.05 million deal from Chelsea and a few own goals and some sloppy timekeeping aside, Sinclair proved to be another good recruit.

EADIE DOES IT

Darren Eadie became the club's first £3 million signing. He joined from Norwich City in December, 1999, an outlay that was equalled six months later when Peter Taylor splashed out to bring in defender Gary Rowett from Birmingham City.

A month after signing Rowett, Taylor made another record signing when he brought striker Ade Akinbiyi to the club from Wolverhampton Wanderers for a £5 million fee. His debut season brought him nine goals in the Premier League as City finished the season 13th after suffering a record-breaking run of eight straight defeats. Akinbiyi made the headlines for all the wrong reasons during the 2001-2002 season. He didn't find the target in the opening nine Premier League games and finally ended the drought with the winning goal against Sunderland in November, 2001. If that didn't silence his critics, the sight of his muscular build when he stripped off his shirt to celebrate must have done. Sadly, he added only one more goal before being sold to Crystal Palace for a fee of £2.2 million.

WHAT A GAME!

Nice ground, shame about the results. Eight minutes into the second half of the 1993 Division One play-off final and a familiar story was unfolding for Leicester City's supporters.

Their sixth appearance at Wembley Stadium was heading for a sixth defeat. Twelve months after Blackburn Rovers inflicted heartbreak, Brian Little's team were back to battle it out with Swindon Town for a place in the Premier League. Swindon player-boss Glenn Hoddle gave his side the lead just before half-time and then two strikes in the space of six minutes just after the interval from Craig Maskell and Shaun Taylor left City trailing 3-0. Incredibly, they wiped out that deficit with three goals in the space of 12 breathless minutes that will never be forgotten by any Leicester supporter among the crowd of 73,802.

Four minutes after Taylor had put Swindon 3-0 ahead, Lee Philpott swung over a high, swirling cross, Steve Walsh smacked a powerful header against the post and Julian Joachim belted home the rebound. Walsh headed home another Philpott cross to make it 3-2 before City drew level. Mike Whitlow led the counter attack with a charging run out of defence and Steve Thompson took his pass in his stride before proving he had the coolest head in the stadium by slipping a sublime shot just inside the far post with the outside of his right boot. Cue absolute pandemonium. City fans cheered, danced and rubbed their eyes in disbelief. But there was to be no happy ending.

With just seven minutes left, Swindon substitute Steve White went down after a challenge from City goalkeeper Kevin Poole and Paul Bodin tucked home the penalty that broke Leicester hearts. City had equalled

the club record of seven straight wins on their way to Wembley.
A 2-1 win over Birmingham City at Filbert Street on February 28th, 1993 was the first of seven consecutive wins.

After the win over the Blues, City hit three goals in each of their next six games and while they ended the season with a 7-1 walloping at Newcastle United, Little's team still finished sixth to set up a two-legged play-off semi-final against Portsmouth. Redevelopment work at Filbert Street meant City had to play their home leg at Nottingham Forest's City Ground and a stunning solo goal from Julian Joachim meant they had the advantage going into the second leg. Ian Ormondroyd and Steve Thompson got the goals in a 2-2 draw at Fratton Park that was enough to send City back to Wembley.

WAS IT A GOAL?

There's never a Russian linesman around when you need one. Mike Newell will tell you all about that. While Nottingham Forest were busy conquering Europe and winning trophies under Brian Clough, City were yo-yoing between the top two divisions, battling relegation, sacking managers and casting envious looks at their flourishing neighbours a few junctions up the M1.

The East Midlands rivals were a division apart when the draw for the fourth round of the League Cup in 1988-89 paired them together at Filbert Street for a game highly anticipated in Leicester.

Although hardly setting Division Two alight, City fans had some cause for optimism. They had beaten the leaders of the top two divisions in the previous rounds. The Foxes followed a 4-1 walloping of Division Two table-toppers Watford with a 2-2 draw at Vicarage Road and then dumped out Norwich City. At the time, the Canaries led Division One, but goals from Newell and Paul Reid ended their interest in the League Cup. Newell and Reid were then key figures in the clash with Forest. Forest full-back Stuart Pearce was sent off for clattering Reid at Filbert Street in front of 26,764 fans while Newell was a whisker away from becoming a Leicester legend. His fierce right-foot shot crashed against the underside of the bar, bounced on the goal line and then away to safety. Or did it? Interviewed almost two decades later, Newell still claimed that the ball had crossed the line and that the goal should have been allowed. It clearly still bothered him. Anyway, the game ended goalless and City were beaten 2-1 in the replay at the City Ground after Paul Groves headed home a Leicester leveller from Newell's cross.

The next meeting between the sides was also in a cup competition. It was in the Northern final of the Zenith Data Systems Cup. Until the arrival of Brian Little in the summer of 1991, City's form in cups had been poor. They had not won a game in the FA Cup for six years, so a run in the Zenith Data Systems competition got pulses racing and they quickened further when the two-legged Northern final meant a clash with Nottingham Forest. The winners would meet the Southern winners at Wembley. City drew 1-1 at Filbert Street with Colin Gordon on target to cancel out Scott Gemmill's opener and Forest won the second leg to end Leicester's hopes. Forest then went on to win the trophy like they usually did back then.

SQUEEZED IN

The 47,298 fans who squeezed into Filbert Street on February 18th, 1928 to watch Leicester City take on Tottenham Hostpur in the fifth round of the FA Cup set a record. It remains the highest attendance at a City home match and that figure does not include the hundreds of fans perched on top of the stands and the supporters who stormed the directors' entrance after the gates were shut. Those that paid to get in raised gate receipts of £4,703 10s 6d and the majority of supporters went home unhappy after City were dumped out 3-0.

THE HIGHEST EVER

The highest gate for a home Football League fixture is the 42,486 that watched the Division One fixture against Arsenal on October 2nd, 1954. City had been promoted to the top flight the previous season as champions and although the opening ten games of the 1954-55 campaign brought only two wins, the visit of Arsenal still attracted a record crowd and they got their money's worth. The sides shared six goals with Arthur Rowley netting twice – including a penalty – and Derek Hines grabbing the other goal for City.

PLENTY OF ROOM

The talents of Gary Lineker, Alan Smith and Kevin MacDonald were not enough to attract more than 6,155 fans through the Filbert Street turnstiles for the visit of Shrewsbury Town on February 22nd, 1983. That remains the lowest post-war attendance for a Leicester City home match and those that were there saw two goals from Lineker, and another from Ian Wilson, secure a 3-2 win that kick-started the Foxes' push for promotion. They put together a 15-game unbeaten run that pipped Fulham for the third promotion spot with the Foxes clinching their return to the top flight with a goalless draw against Burnley at Filbert Street on the final day of the season. There were 29,453 fans present to see a game that took place just over 11 weeks after the clash with Shrewsbury.

A LOW ATTENDANCE

The lowest attendance for a First Division fixture at Filbert Street was the 7,237 that watched City battle out a 2-2 draw with West Bromwich Albion on October 12th, 1985.

WORTH THE WAIT

Leicester City took on Sheffield United in the 1961 FA Cup semi-final at Elland Road. And, 234 minutes after the game kicked off, there was a goal!

City set off on the long road to Wembley with a 3-1 win over Oxford United at Filbert Street that was followed by a 5-1 battering of Bristol City. The result set up a fifth-round clash with Birmingham City that went to a replay settled by Ken Leek's double. He was the match-winner again in the quarter-final replay against Barnsley.

City were drawn against the Blades in the last four – and the teams came up with a cure for insomnia. There were no goals when they met at Leeds United's Elland Road and five days later, the sides fought out another 0-0 draw at St. Andrew's in a game that went to extra time. The wait for a goal looked set to end 11 minutes into the third meeting at the City Ground in Nottingham when City were awarded a penalty, but Ian King stubbed his foot into the ground at the moment of impact and the chance was gone. It was left to Jimmy Walsh to grab the tie's opening goal.

He headed home 24 minutes into the third meeting between the sides and Leek doubled the lead just after the interval. The Blades were handed a route back into the game when they were awarded a 65th-minute penalty, but Graham Shaw pulled his effort wide and the opportunity was lost. City went on to lose the final 2-0 to Tottenham Hotspur.

SEVEN UP

During the 1974-75 season, City and Arsenal met an incredible seven times! Arsenal were 1-0 winners at Filbert Street on the opening day of the season and the sides were paired together the following month in the League Cup. City went through 2-1 in a replay after a goalless draw at Highbury and after another 0-0 scoreline in the return fixture in Division One, the draw for the fifth round of the FA Cup paired them together again after the Foxes had scraped past non-league Leatherhead. After a goalless draw at Highbury, the replay ended 1-1 after extra time and that set up a third meeting. Arsenal went through to the quarter-finals with a 1-0 win in front of their home fans.

WHAT A SIGNING!

Gerry Daly headed off down the M69 to join Leicester City from Coventry City and the Foxes were soon heading for promotion. Daly, a slender, stylish midfielder formerly at Manchester United, joined in February, 1983 and played all 17 remaining games of the season; City only lost once. He made his debut in a 1-0 win at Carlisle United and following a defeat at Grimsby Town, City put together a 15-game unbeaten run that enabled them to pip Fulham for the third automatic promotion spot. Daly, so accurate with his passing it was as though he had telescopic sights strapped to his boots, was called up by the Republic of Ireland while on loan at City and his only goal for the Foxes was a sweetly struck right-foot shot from the edge of the penalty area that completed a 5-0 drubbing of promotion rivals Wolverhampton

Wanderers. There was much surprise and disappointment among Leicester supporters when Milne decided against trying to make Daly's move to Leicester permanent during the summer. Instead, he went on to join Derby County for £300,000.

GOAL-HUNGRY FRYATT

Matty Fryatt was another inspired signing. He joined from Walsall in January, 2006 and made his debut as a substitute in a 2-1 defeat at Sheffield Wednesday. That result left Robert Kelly's side just one place and one point above the drop zone in the second tier of English football, but in the space of four days, Fryatt helped fire his new team to safety. He was on target in the 3-2 win at Queens Park Rangers and followed it with the winner against Wolverhampton Wanderers at the Walkers Stadium. Fryatt ended the season with six goals and City survived.

KEV TO THE RESCUE

Leicester were one place off the bottom of Division Two in November, 1989 when boss David Pleat brought in Kevin Campbell on loan from Arsenal and the teenage striker's five goals in 11 games were crucial in securing City's survival. His strikes included a stunning long-range winner at Portsmouth on New Year's Day and Campbell was given an emotional send off at Filbert Street after his final game. He went on to win the Football League, FA Cup, League Cup and European Cup Winners' Cup with the Gunners.

LAST ORDERS

In the summer of 1930, The Turk's Head on Welford Road gained a new landlord and Leicester City lost a legend. City's board were not impressed by John Duncan's plan to combine his playing career with running the hostelry and the fall out spelled the end for him at Filbert Street after 295 games and 95 goals. Duncan was approached by several clubs, but was intent on his career in the licensed trade. He had joined City along with brother Tom from Scottish club Raith Rovers for a fee of £1,500 in the summer of 1922. Leicester boss Peter Hodge knew all about Duncan having previously been his manager at Raith and City fans soon discovered why he was so highly rated. Known as 'Tokey', Duncan netted twice on his debut at Stockport County in a 5-4 win and ended his first season at the club with 20 goals. The only game he missed was the trip to Bury on the last day of the season when a 2-0 loss cost City the chance of being promoted.

Leicester went up as champions in 1924-25 and Duncan had a starring role. He netted 30 goals, including six in the 7-0 thumping of Port Vale on Christmas Day after Arthur Chandler had opened the scoring for the Foxes. Duncan went on to be a key player in the side that were runners-up behind Sheffield Wednesday in Division One in the 1928-29 season and was an ever-present with 40 appearances the following season as City finished eighth. After that, Duncan left Filbert Street and headed off to the pub. He stayed involved in football with Leicester Thursday League side Solaris, then Leicester Nomads, and in August, 1940, Duncan became a founder committee member of the City Supporters' Club. He was named City's manager in March, 1946 following Tom Bromilow's departure and went on to lead Leicester out at Wembley in the 1949 FA Cup Final against Wolverhampton Wanderers. The game ended in defeat and a few months later Duncan left City after a bust up with the board over transfer policy and headed back to the pub. He died in Leicester in March, 1966 at the age of 70. His brother Tom made 42 appearances for City – scoring six goals – and moved on after being unable to dislodge Hughie Adcock. A third Duncan brother, Jim, played in the Scottish League with Lochgelly United, their uncle David Bain played for Heart of Midlothian and cousin Jack Bain appeared for Dunfermline and Dundee United.

CRAZY STUFF

In the early days of Leicester Fosse, there were some bizarre goings on… A match against Coalville in November, 1886 ended before the final whistle when Fosse's Leicestershire rivals were so disgusted with a decision by the umpire that they stormed off the pitch in protest and refused to return to complete the fixture!

Later that month, Fosse turned up for a match at Belgrave with only 10 players and ended up plucking a supporter out of the crowd to play for them! Fosse still ran out 2-0 winners in the big Leicester derby. At the start of the 1887-88 season, the Belgrave Road Sports Ground became Fosse's home ground. The venue had been built seven years earlier by local entrepreneur Colonel Barnaby and while the impressive facilities included athletics and cycle tracks around a playing area big enough to be used as a cricket pitch, there was nowhere for the players to change. That meant they had to get changed before matches and later have their post-match wash at the White Hart Hotel that was almost a mile away from the ground. Fosse only stayed there for one season, however. The city's rugby union team, Leicester Tigers, outbid them for the use of the ground.

A FIRST

The game against Burton Swifts in November, 1897 became the first fixture when supporters had to pay an admission fee and they got their money's worth as Fosse were 3-2 winners through goals from Billy Dorrell, Willie Freebairn and Johnny McMillan. Presumably, supporters were offered a refund after Castle Donington didn't turn up for a fixture the following month. Instead, Fosse played their reserves in a practice match that ended in a 1-1 draw.

DRESSING FOR THE OCCASION

It was so cold when Fosse took on Doncaster Rovers in a Midland League fixture in November, 1893 that goalkeeper Jimmy Thraves took to the field wearing an overcoat! The snow became so bad that the game was eventually abandoned by the referee.

RED CARDS

The pantomime season came early in 1962. Oh yes it did. Leicester City took on Aston Villa at Filbert Street on December 8th, 1962 and after just 15 seconds, Len Chalmers put the ball in the net. The wrong net. Derek Dougan, who went on to play for City, launched the ball forward for his strikers to chase, Leicester defender Chalmers got there first and lobbed over goalkeeper Gordon Banks to gift Villa the lead. City fought back to grab a 3-3 draw with David Gibson netting twice and Mike Stringfellow getting the other.

IN THE FRAME

Willie Frame had the misfortune to score an own goal on his Leicester debut. Frame, signed from junior football in Glasgow, was handed his first start for Leicester at Tottenham Hotspur on October 6th, 1934 and his own goal in the last minute meant the home side escaped with a point from a 2-2 draw. Danny Liddle and Arthur Maw were on target for City at White Hart Lane.

DOUBLE CLANGER

Leicester defenders Colin Appleton and Ian King were the match winners in City's match at Burnley in September, 1961 – but for the Clarets rather than City! They both scored own goals to clinch a 2-0 win for the Clarets in the Division One fixture at Turf Moor.

ASSISTING THE BAGGIES

John Sjoberg scored two own goals against City for West Bromwich Albion at the Hawthorns on April 22nd, 1966. His blunders helped the Baggies to a 5-1 win.

CRUISING FOR THE RECORD BOOKS

Pat Kruse only made two appearances for City, in the last two games of the 1973-74 season, and went into the record books after leaving Filbert Street. He lined up for Torquay United against Cambridge United in a Division Four fixture on January 3rd, 1977 and netted the quickest own goal ever recorded in the Football League. There were just six seconds on the clock when Kruse put Cambridge ahead. Although his City career was brief, Kruse went on to make more than 300 appearances for clubs including Brentford, Northampton and Barnet.

STAYING PUT

Leicester City were crowned Division Two champions in 1956-57 and it didn't look like they were going to hang around in the top tier. The following season, City lost six of their opening seven games shrugging off the horror start to survive and go on to spend 12 successive seasons in Division One. That remains the longest spell the Foxes have spent in the top division of English football with their best finish being fourth in 1962-63 when they were on course for a league and FA Cup double until it all fell apart. City reached three FA Cup Finals during that spell and lifted the League Cup in 1964. They were relegated in 1969 three weeks after defeat in the FA Cup Final against Manchester City.

TEN AT THE TOP

City spent a decade in Division One between 1925 and 1935 and in 1928-29 achieved their highest-ever league placing when they finished second behind Sheffield Wednesday.

SEVENTH IN SEVEN

Jimmy Bloomfield put together a team that spent seven seasons in the top flight (1971-78), achieving a best finish of seventh in 1975-76.

STEADY

Martin O'Neill took City back into the Premier League in May, 1996 and the Foxes went on to enjoy six seasons in the top flight. City finished in the top ten for four successive seasons before O'Neill left for Celtic in the summer of 2000. Peter Taylor briefly took the Foxes to the top of the Premier League in October, 2000 and City were relegated at the end of the following season.

OVER ONE HUNDRED YEARS AGO...

The club's first taste of top-flight football was short lived. Leicester Fosse kicked off the 1908-09 season in Division One with a 1-1 draw against Sheffield Wednesday in front of around 16,000 fans at Filbert Street. Fosse had to wait until the fourth game of the season to register their first win at Preston North End, but a spell of 14 games without a win left them rooted to the bottom of the table and they stayed there.

WATERS DEBUT

"Oh yes for the youngster!" screamed excitable *Match of the Day* commentator Barry Davies and Joe Waters entered Leicester City folklore. Jimmy Bloomfield's City had drawn comparisons to Brazil in their 4-0 win at Luton Town in the fifth round of the FA Cup in 1974. The win set up a quarter-final tie at Queens Park Rangers where Bloomfield was without the injured Alan Birchenall and Alan Woollett for the trip to Loftus Road, so he handed a debut to Waters and the 21-year-old more than justified his selection. City were under pressure in the first half with Stan Bowles driving Rangers on but hit back to take the lead after the break through Waters. The ball ran to him 20 yards out and he sent his curving right-foot shot beyond Phil Parkes' fingertips and into the corner of the net. It would later be voted 'Goal of the Month' by *Match of the Day* viewers and there was more to come from Waters. He added the decisive second following a breathtaking counter attack.

City belted clear from a corner, Frank Worthington broke away and squared for Waters to lift the ball over the advancing Parkes. Waters was plastered all over the newspapers and then got the chance to repeat his heroics against Liverpool in the FA Cup semi-final at Old Trafford. City, who would have preferred to draw Newcastle United or Burnley in the last four, had a lucky escape when Kevin Keegan hit the post in the closing minutes. Waters was missing from the side that lined up for the replay at Villa Park. Liverpool were 3-1 victors – Len Glover was on target for the Foxes – to go through to the final.

PEAKING TOO EARLY

Waters' reward for his performance at Rangers earned him a call up to the Republic of Ireland squad, but the chunky midfielder could not build on his astonishing start to his City career. After his debut, he went on to make only 15 more appearances and added only one more goal before leaving for Grimsby Town. He went on to be a Mariners legend in a career that spanned 357 league games which included a club-record run of 226 consecutive appearances. Waters then took on a player-coach role with Tacoma Stars in America's Major League Soccer where his team-mates included Keith Weller.

SWINDON FUN

The next time Leicester City meet Swindon Town, you really want to be there. There was the 1993 Division One play-off final when City wiped out a 3-0 deficit before being pipped in a seven-goal thriller. Five seasons earlier, Leicester had served up another unforgettable match at Filbert Street. City were heading for defeat when they trailed 2-0 with around 10 minutes left and, after Paul Ramsey and Steve Walsh had levelled the scores, the Foxes found an unlikely match winner. Mark Venus, for so long the target of terrace derision, walloped home an unstoppable left-foot volley from 25 yards into the top corner and the game was won. The following season, Swindon opened up a 3-0 lead at Filbert Street and City clawed their way back to earn a point with Gary McAllister on target twice.

GOAL FEST

City had a dramatic late escape in the first leg of their League Cup tie with Brentford in September, 1984. They produced a four-goal flurry in the last nine minutes to overturn Brentford's 2-0 lead with the goals coming from John O'Neill, Ian Banks, Steve Lynex and Gary Lineker. Two weeks later, City won the second leg 2-0 at Griffin Park to go through 6-2 on aggregate.

DUTCH TOUCH

City were heading for a third-round exit from the FA Cup in January, 2006 when Tottenham Hotspur opened up a 2-0 lead against Craig Levein's Championship strugglers in front of the *Match of the Day* cameras. Elvis Hammond handed City a lifeline and then Stephen Hughes slammed home the leveller before Mark De Vries rolled home the winner deep into injury time.

THREE IN THIRTEEN

Perhaps the most satisfying comeback of all came at Villa Park in February, 1995. Three months earlier, Brian Little had walked out on City to take charge of Aston Villa and his new side led Leicester 4-1 with just 13 minutes left. Iwan Roberts started the fightback by heading home a Mike Galloway cross and David Lowe pulled another back to set up a thrilling climax. The game was deep into injury time when Lowe forced home Colin Hill's header to snatch a point.

REED ALL ABOUT IT

Leicester City crashed out of the FA Cup and the nation was outraged. Referee Mike Reed's decision to award a spot-kick to Chelsea in the dying moments of extra time at the end of the FA Cup fifth-round replay in February, 1997 dominated headlines, radio phone-ins and even Prime Minister's Question Time.

The injustice felt by City was shared by supporters across the country. Leicester had been incensed by comments made by Chelsea boss Ruud Gullit after the 2-2 draw at Filbert Street ten days earlier. His claim that Leicester had been lucky to force a replay – through goals from Steve Walsh and an own goal after they had trailed 2-0 – did not go down well with Martin O'Neill.

City's manager didn't feel like a lucky man when he looked at his team's injury list and there was still the second leg of the Coca-Cola Cup semi-final against Wimbledon to come. To compound matters, they were drawn against the favourites for the FA Cup after reaching the last 16 with wins over Southend United and Norwich City. Early exits for Manchester United, Arsenal, Liverpool, Newcastle and Aston Villa meant Chelsea were fancied to end a spell of 27 years without a trophy by lifting the cup. City's late fightback at Filbert Street in a game televised live on the BBC denied them a place in the quarter-finals and O'Neill's team were similarly spirited in the replay at Stamford Bridge. The score was goalless after 90 minutes and stayed that way heading into the dying moments of extra time. Then it happened. Chelsea striker Erland Johnsen tried to burst through a gap between Leicester defenders Matt Elliott and Spencer Prior and took a tumble. Referee Reed pointed to the spot and City's protests were echoed by armchair fans around the country when Sky Sports replays showed no contact had been made. That night, BBC Radio Five Live's Danny Baker spoke for the nation when he opined: "It was scandalous, an absolute scandal." And, there was more to follow. Tabloid headlines screamed 'The Worst Referee In The World', a Leicester fan tried to claim damages because the stress of his side's controversial exit had affected his health and made him take time off work and Prime Minister John Major spoke in defence of his team Chelsea.

Chelsea went on to win the cup and more than a decade later, *The Guardian* remembered the penalty award that went against Leicester as one of the worst refereeing decisions ever made.

WHAT A HERBERT

Leicester Fosse took the unusual step of handing goalkeeper Herbert Bown the job of penalty taker in the 1916-1917 season. Bown repaid the faith placed in him by netting Fosse's goal in a 2-1 defeat at Hull City in March, 1917. He was an ever-present between the posts for Fosse that season, but lost the job of penalty-taker during the following campaign. In October, 1917 he missed a spot-kick against Sheffield Wednesday at Filbert Street and that proved to be decisive as the Owls headed home with maximum points from a 2-1 win. Bown was never allowed to take another penalty for the club, but he was soon back in the headlines.

Two weeks after that penalty miss against Wednesday, Bown was involved in another bizarre incident. As he was lining up to take a goal kick in the match at Bradford City, a dog ran onto the pitch unnoticed by the Fosse keeper and he booted the canine rather than the ball! Fortunately, the dog was not badly hurt. Fosse went on to lose the match 4-1. Bown had previously played for Essex as an amateur before joining Fosse in April, 1913. At the end of the season, he set off with the squad on their historic tour of Sweden and was between the posts in the five games that included a pair of wins over the Swedish national team. Bown went on to enter the club's record books in the 1919-1920 season for keeping a club-record seven successive clean sheets in league fixtures. The run started with a 2-0 win over Stockport County on February 7th in a Division Two fixture and Bown did not concede another goal until April 3rd when Bury snatched a 1-0 win.

After nine years with Fosse, Bown left the club in May, 1922. He made 266 appearances for Leicester – including 112 during World War Two – and a goal from the penalty spot. He went on to join Halifax Town and got on the score-sheet for the Shaymen during two ever-present seasons with them. Bown was then put up for sale at the bargain price of £350, but no clubs expressed an interest and he ended up returning to Leicester to run a fish and poultry business. He was then brought out of retirement in January, 1925 to play four games for Hull City after they were hit by an injury crisis. Bown died in Leicester in February, 1959 at the age of 65.

CRAZY DAYS

Leicester Fosse marked their entry into the Football League with a bizarre seven-goal thriller at Grimsby Town. The clash at Grimsby's Abbey Park on September 1st, 1894 ended in a 4-3 defeat for Fosse and was followed by some revelations from the home side's goalkeeper. Whitehouse reckoned that the referee had not noticed a shot from Fosse player Priestman had crossed the line and that McArthur's legitimate goal for Fosse had been scored while the Grimsby keeper was pulling up his socks.

New signing David Skea went into the record books as Fosse's first-ever goal scorer in a Football League fixture and it was an own goal by Harry Bailey that proved to be the decisive strike in the match. Fosse recorded their first win in their next fixture. McArthur opened the scoring after seven minutes against Rotherham Town and Skea added a hat-trick to complete a 4-2 win at Walnut Street. Fosse ended the season in fourth place and the reserves lifted the Wellingborough Cup and Leics & Northants League championship.

William D. Clark came to Leicester Fosse in the summer of 1897 and brought with him some fairly bonkers ideas. Clark took on the secretary/manager role having previously held a similar post at both Burton Wanderers and Derby County and was always looking for ways to stir up some publicity. He helped arrange an exhibition baseball match between Crystal Palace and Derby County in August, 1897 and then came up with the idea of a series of 100-yard handicap races for footballers. Billy Dorrell, in his second spell with Fosse after rejoining from Aston Villa, was the winner and he also took part in the rather unusual pre-match entertainment before the home game against Darwen in February, 1898. Clark arranged a 440-yard challenge race between Dorrell and American half-miler C. H. Kilpatrick that the Fosse flyer won. His victory earned him £10, cemented his hero status at Leicester and did nothing to help Fosse. Dorrell must still have been out of puff when the opening whistle blew of the match with Darwen and the visitors left Filbert Street with a 1-0 win. A week later, the club's board had to clamp down on unruly behaviour by some players. They indefinitely suspended six players following alcohol-related incidents and several of them never played in the Football League again.

DREAM DEBUTS

If there's such a thing as a dream debut, then this is it… At the age of 16 years and 192 days, Dave Buchanan became City's youngest-ever player when he made his debut against Oldham Athletic at Filbert Street on January 1st, 1979. Not content with that feat, he then found the target in a 2-0 win to make him the youngest-ever goalscorer in the Foxes' history. Sadly, he never built on that tremendous start to his Leicester career and added only seven more goals.

THINGS CHANGE…

At the time, the signing of Arthur Rowley wasn't well received by Leicester City fans. They liked Jack Lee and Rowley was brought in to replace him. Rowley, a £14,000 signing from Fulham, set about winning over his public by scoring plenty of goals. His first came on his debut in August, 1950 and secured a 3-2 win at Bury.

UNLUCKY

Robert Ullathorne's Leicester City debut lasted all of 11 minutes. With City boss Martin O'Neill's squad decimated by injuries he brought in the former Norwich City stopper from Spanish club CA Osasuna in February, 1997. Ullathorne was handed his Foxes debut in the first leg of the Coca-Cola Cup semi-final against Wimbledon at Filbert Street but suffered a broken ankle after just 11 minutes of the goalless draw and didn't play for City again for 22 months.

A FLYING START

A few days after becoming Leicester City's record signing, Mike Newell showed why Bryan Hamilton had splashed out £350,000 to bring the striker to Filbert Street. Newell made his debut against Oldham Athletic in September, 1987 and his flying header sent City on their way to a 4–1 win at Filbert Street that ended a run of three straight defeats.

NOT AS GOOD AS HIS BROTHER

Newell's departure to Everton led to Wayne Clarke moving in the opposite direction. He marked his City debut with a goal at Hull City on the opening day of the 1989-90 season... but only scored one more for Leicester.

MORE DREAM DEBUTS

And here are a few more memorable debuts...

Who needs Gary Lineker? Leicester City's team-sheet for the penultimate game of the 1982-83 season at Oldham Athletic was missing the 26-goal striker. In stepped teenager Robert Jones for his debut. Also ruled out at Boundary Park were Steve Lynex and Ian Wilson for a match that could make or break City's promotion hopes. Gordon Milne's team had jumped into the third promotion place in Division Two for the first time that season with a 2-2 draw at Leeds United seven days earlier and more than 5,000 Leicester fans headed up to Oldham hoping to see them stay there.

Jones, who played for England Schoolboys and then won youth caps with Wales, went close with a long-range effort and then put City ahead three minutes before the break. He raced onto Kevin MacDonald's through ball and coolly squeezed his left-foot shot just inside the goalkeeper's near post. Jones was still beaming with joy when the game restarted and there was more reason to smile nine minutes into the second half when Paul Ramsey doubled Leicester's lead. Although Oldham pulled a goal back, the Foxes held on to their advantage and went on to secure promotion. The following season, Jones helped City secure their first top-flight point with a goal in a 2-2 draw against Stoke City in the seventh fixture, but made a total of just 17 appearances and scored three goals before being released.

IMMEDIATE IMPACT

Mark Yeates didn't take long to make an impact at Leicester. He arrived on loan from Tottenham Hotspur in January, 2007 and two days later, he made his debut against Luton Town in a Championship fixture at the Walkers Stadium. Six minutes after kick-off, he was celebrating a goal. Yeates was on hand to tuck home the loose ball after Iain Hume's shot had been blocked by goalkeeper Marlon Beresford. The game ended 1-1 and Yeates made only eight more appearances for City before returning to White Hart Lane and then making a permanent switch to Colchester United.

SIXTH ROUND

Then there is Joe Waters and his two-goal debut in the FA Cup quarter-final at Queens Park Rangers in 1974 that is mentioned elsewhere.

DERBY DAYS

The big local derby got underway in glorious sunshine – and it was all over 15 minutes later! That was how long it took Martin O'Neill's Leicester City to net four times at Derby County in April, 1998 in front of the Sky Sports cameras. City were ahead within two minutes with Emile Heskey powering home a header from Steve Guppy's cross and 46 seconds after the restart, the lead was doubled. Steve Claridge picked up a misplaced pass and sent Heskey racing away down the right who sent a cross into the penalty area for Muzzy Izzet to arrive at the right time to head into the roof of the net. Heskey added number three from Guppy's corner after just nine minutes and the scoring was completed with 15 minutes played. Robbie Savage swung over a cross from the right and Ian Marshall got above his marker to steer his header into the corner of the net. And that was that.

MARSHALL MATTERS

Marshall had been the hat-trick hero for City when the sides met at Filbert Street the previous season. City were without Neil Lennon, Heskey and Izzet and fell behind to an early strike from Dean Sturridge,

MUZZY IZZET CELEBRATES.

who went on to play for Leicester. Marshall then netted three times in the space of just 21 first-half minutes to put the Foxes in charge and after Sturridge pulled a goal back, Claridge put the game beyond Derby in the 58th minute with a close-range finish.

SIX IN THIRTY

Leicester striker Iwan Roberts bagged a hat-trick in just 11 minutes in an astonishing six-goal thriller against Derby at Filbert Street in April, 1994. All the goals came in the opening half hour. Derby were 2-0 ahead in 12 minutes through former Fox Paul Kitson and a Jimmy Willis strike before Roberts' treble blast after 17, 22 and 28 minutes. A minute after Roberts had put City in front, Kitson levelled the scores.

GARY PITCHES IN

Gary Lineker also scored a hat-trick in the big East Midlands derby. His goal treble came in the 4-0 win at the Baseball Ground in October, 1983 and strike partner Alan Smith got the other.

WHITE TIGHTS

Ever the showman, Keith Weller left his audience wanting more... He took the Filbert Street stage on January 6th, 1979 resplendent in white tights and then dazzled his opponents, the crowd and a television audience of millions in an FA Cup third-round tie against Norwich City. A few weeks after that, it was all over.

Weller's goalscoring swansong owed much to a hot-air pitch cover that meant City's game was one of only three fixtures to survive the big freeze and BBC TV's cameras were there to capture all the drama for the *Match of the Day* viewers. They saw Weller take to the pitch wearing white tights and then go on to score City's second goal in a 3-0 win. It proved to be Weller's last goal for City. Two weeks later, he played in the 1-1 draw against Blackburn Rovers at Filbert Street and never played for the club again.

He had arrived at Leicester from Chelsea for a £100,000 fee as boss Jimmy Bloomfield set about putting together one of the most exciting teams in City's history. Weller made his debut for the Foxes in a goalless draw against Crystal Palace in October, 1971 and among his five top-flight goals in his first season was a stunning solo effort in a 2-1 win at East Midlands rivals Nottingham Forest. There would be many more highlights.

In November, 1973 he belted home an unstoppable volley from the edge of the penalty area to secure victory over Newcastle United at Filbert Street. His sparkling midfield promptings helped carve out many of Frank Worthington's 24 goals in all competitions as City finished the season ninth in Division One and reached the semi-finals of the FA Cup where they bowed out to Liverpool after a replay. Weller's goal at Luton Town in the fifth round of the FA Cup was among his best and was voted Goal of the Season by ITV viewers. His form also earned him four England caps at the end of the season and he bagged the winner against Northern Ireland in May, 1974 with a rare header. Frustratingly, he never got the chance to add more caps and his refusal to come out for the second half of a fixture against Ipswich Town in December, 1974 showed his frustration at City's inability to fulfill their potential. Weller went on to play in America and tragically died in the States in November, 2004 at the age of 58 after losing his battle with cancer.

ENDING THE JINX

Until May 30th, 1994, Wembley meant only one thing to Leicester City, and that was heartbreak.

City's six previous games at the home of football had all ended in defeat. They had lost four FA Cup Finals and then suffered back-to-back losses in play-off finals against Blackburn Rovers and Swindon Town. Brian Little took his team back to Wembley for the third successive season in May, 1994 to face East Midlands rivals Derby County with a place in the Premier League at stake.

City had finished fourth in the table after ending the season with a nine-game unbeaten run and edged out Tranmere Rovers in the play-off semi-finals. Simon Grayson's goal-line handball in the first leg at Tranmere was seen by everyone at Prenton Park apart from the officials to ensure the scoreline was blank going into the return at Filbert Street. Little stunned

City's fans when he included Steve Walsh in the starting line-up. Walsh had suffered a cruciate ligament injury in a 2-0 defeat at Middlesbrough the previous September and his return to the side seven months later in a 1-1 draw at Watford proved to be short-lived. He was back for the second leg against Tranmere and despite clearly not being fully match fit, he had a hand in Ian Ormondroyd's opener. Rovers levelled and David Speedie grabbed the goal that sent City back to Wembley.

He didn't get the chance to play there, however. The Scot was sent off in the dying moments following a bust up with Rovers keeper Eric Nixon and banned for the final against Derby.

Iwan Roberts stepped in to replace Speedie and partner Walsh up front, but most of the early action was at the other end of the pitch and it was no surprise when Tommy Johnson fired the Rams into the lead after outpacing City's defence. Leicester were level when Gary Coatsworth walloped the ball skywards and Walsh out-jumped Rams keeper Martin Taylor to head in.

The goal probably should have been ruled out for a foul on the keeper and definitely should have been cleared by Derby defender Paul Williams on the goal-line. Instead, City went into the break on level terms and then grabbed the winner, and their place in the Premier League, with four minutes left. Ian Ormondroyd met Simon Grayson's right-wing cross with a header that Taylor could not hang on to, and Walsh was on hand to tap home the loose ball and end the Foxes' Wembley jinx.

PAYING THE PENALTY

You could have cut the tension with a tub of lard. Leicester City beat Huddersfield Town and Charlton Athletic in the Simod Cup in 1987-88 to set up a third-round home date with Stoke City that attracted a crowd of just 5,161. It went all the way to a penalty shoot-out after two goalless hours and David Pleat's team fancied their chances. Between the posts they had Paul Cooper, who had saved a penalty during the match and kept out eight of ten spot-kicks he faced when playing for Ipswich Town in the 1979-80 season. But he didn't stop any in the shootout against Stoke. City went out 5-3 with Mike Newell missing the crucial spot-kick after Gary McAllister, Peter Weir and Mark Venus found the back of the net. "Someone had to miss," said Newell afterwards, "or we would have been there all night!"

UP FOR GRABS

There were priceless Premier League points at stake when Leicester and Manchester City squared up at the Walkers Stadium on April 24th, 2004. The sides were level at 1-1 when Leicester were awarded a penalty with just nine minutes left after Muzzy Izzet was felled by Tarnat. Paul Dickov, already a Manchester City legend for his last-gasp heroics in the 1999 play-off final against Gillingham, had his spot-kick saved by David James. Seven days later, Leicester's 2-2 draw at Charlton Athletic wasn't enough to keep them in the top division. Dickov was more accurate from the penalty spot when he lined up against City the following season. He got the only goal of the FA Cup quarter-final for Blackburn Rovers at Ewood Park in the 82nd minute after City defender Darren Kenton had brought down Morten Gamst Pedersen.

THE DREADED DROP

Iain Hume was another Leicester hero who missed a crucial spot-kick. He was off target in the clash with Sheffield Wednesday at the Walkers Stadium in April, 2008 that Leicester went into knowing victory would secure their survival. Hume missed the chance to level the scores at 2-2 and City went on to be beaten 3-1 by the Owls. They suffered relegation to the third tier of English football for the first time in their history eight days later.

THEY HAD 12 MEN

Leicester Fosse were up against it at Burslem Port Vale in April, 1892. They took to the pitch with only ten men after Owen missed his train and after the referee also failed to show, a spectator was plucked from the crowd to do the job. Fosse were beaten 2-0 and protested that the official had been far from impartial. The Midland League ordered the game to be replayed. Fosse had 11 men for the fixture next time and there was a neutral referee – but it didn't do them any good. They were beaten 4-0.

PLAY IT AGAIN

Fosse's 6-0 thumping of Derby Junction at Walnut Street in March, 1893 was also scrubbed from the record books. The sides had met in Leicester a few weeks earlier and while Derby had agreed to cede home advantage, neither club checked the fixture switch had the approval of the Midland League. So, the game was played again in Derby and Fosse ran out 3-1 winners.

WHAT A PICTURE!

The decision to make that 6-0 win over Derby void meant Alf Slack had his hat-trick wiped from the record books and 92 years later, the same thing happened to Leicester legend Gary Lineker.

The draw for the third round of the FA Cup in 1985 handed City a trip to Burton Albion and the home side decided to stage the game at Derby County's Baseball Ground to pull in a bigger crowd. Burton sniffed an upset when David Vaughan put them ahead midway through the first half. City levelled and then came the incident that put both clubs in the headlines for the wrong reasons. Leicester and Derby fans clashed behind the goal and a missile was thrown which hit Burton goalkeeper Paul Evans on the head. He carried on after treatment, but later said he remembered nothing of the five goals that flew past him after he was struck. The FA ordered the game to be replayed – meaning Lineker's hat-trick no longer stood – and the sides met behind closed doors at Coventry City's Highfield Road. Paul Ramsey got the only goal of the game and the only cheers came from a pair of City fans who had managed to convince officials they were photographers!

THRASHINGS

Everyone knows – well, everyone reading this anyway – that Leicester City's record win is the 10-0 pasting they dished out to Portsmouth at Filbert Street in October, 1928. But the Foxes have recorded a couple of bigger victories in their history. In October, 1894, Fosse put 13 goals past Notts Olympic without reply in an FA Cup qualifying match with 'Tout' Miller and Willie McArthur grabbing four apiece. David Skea grabbed a hat-trick for Fosse and Johnny Hill netted twice.

A DELIGHTFUL DOZEN

Then there was the 12-1 thumping of Syston Wreake Valley in November, 1888 in a first round tie in the Leicestershire Association Challenge Cup. Harry Webb got six of them a month after becoming the club's first professional when he joined from Stafford Rangers.

A HAT-TRICK OF NINES

Leicester have put nine goals past their opponents three times. They were 9-1 winners over Walsall Town Swifts in January, 1895 with David Skea and Bob Gordon both grabbing two goals apiece and Gainsborough Trinity were walloped 9-1 in December, 1909. Dave Walker led the rout with four goals and Fred Shinton fired home a hat-trick. City smashed home nine goals again at Filbert Street in November, 1953. Lincoln City were on the receiving end of a 9-2 thrashing. Derek Hines netted five times for the Foxes and Arthur Rowley was on target twice – including a penalty. City's record away win came at Coventry City on the day Foxes legend Ken Keyworth completed a switch to Highfield Road. He saw his former team storm to an 8-1 win in a League Cup fifth-round tie over the Sky Blues in December, 1964 – despite being without goalkeeper Gordon Banks for a spell. An injury to Banks led to Graham Cross going between the posts and he was seldom troubled as City went on the rampage. Full-back Richie Norman was on target twice for City and they were collector's items. He scored just five times in 365 appearances for Leicester. Sky Blues skipper George Curtis added an own goal and City went on to lift the trophy with victory over Stoke City in the two-legged final.

SUPER STEVIE

Leicester City legend Steve Claridge followed the best goal of his career with the most stupid thing he has ever said! Time was running out in the Division One play-off final between Martin O'Neill's City and Crystal Palace at Wembley in May, 1996. The game was just seconds away from a penalty shoot-out when Palace failed to clear a free kick, the ball dropped to Claridge and he sent his shot into the top corner and the Foxes back into the Premier League. The final whistle blew just seconds later and then Claridge stunned the millions watching by saying on television that the winning goal had gone in off his shin!

"I was just trying to make a joke," remembered Claridge, "and I wish I hadn't done it now. It was probably the most stupid thing I've ever said. I hit the ball as sweet as a nut. It was the best goal of my career."

Eight weeks earlier, Claridge had kick-started City's promotion charge at Charlton Athletic after begging O'Neill not to be dropped. Claridge did not exactly set Filbert Street alight following his £1 million move from Birmingham City. His debut at Ipswich Town, which ended in a 4-2 defeat, was memorable only for the way his name was misspelt on the back of his shirt – with an extra 'r' – and he drew a blank in his first six games for City. Claridge remembers pleading with O'Neill to give him another chance at Charlton Athletic and he repaid his manager with the only goal of the game. Four days later, City were 1-0 winners at Crystal Palace and the charge into the play-offs was underway. City ended the season with four straight wins to set up a play-off semi-final against Stoke City. The sides battled out a goalless draw at Filbert Street and Garry Parker bagged the only goal in the Potteries to send Leicester through to Wembley. They fell behind to Andy Roberts' first-half strike for Palace and had to wait until the 76th minute to level.

Parker kept his cool from the penalty spot after Muzzy Izzet had been felled by Marc Edworthy, who went on to play for City a decade later. Parker then had a hand in City's winner that came just seconds after O'Neill had stunned Leicester fans by replacing goalkeeper Kevin Poole with Zeljko 'Spider' Kalac in anticipation of a penalty shoot-out. Parker's free kick was nodded down by Julian Watts and Claridge's shin did the rest.

KOP THAT!

Ten minutes after coming on for his Leicester City debut at Liverpool, Graham Fenton was celebrating in front of a bunch of cranes and steel girders. Fenton's goal put the Foxes 2-0 ahead in front of the Kop in August, 1997, but rebuilding work at that end of the ground meant there were no supporters in one of the most famous stands in world football and no City fans there to see it. Matt Elliott had earlier put Leicester in

front after just 72 seconds and with seven minutes left, Fenton tapped home number two after goalkeeper David James had failed to hang onto Emile Heskey's shot. Paul Ince rifled home a late goal for the Reds that came too late to prevent City starting their Premier League campaign with back-to-back wins. That was about as good as it got for Fenton, a £1.1 million signing from Blackburn Rovers. He netted only four more goals for City before leaving for Walsall.

FIRST REPLACEMENT

Paul Groves was the first City substitute to find the target after stepping off the bench. Groves, a £12,000 signing from Burton Albion where he combined playing with his job as a bricklayer, came on in the penultimate game of the 1987-88 season against Huddersfield Town. He marked the occasion by powering home a header in a 3-0 win as David Pleat's team ended the Division Two season with a flourish. Groves only scored once more for City – a header in the League Cup fourth-round replay at Nottingham Forest the following season – and went on to play for several clubs including Grimsby Town, where he also managed.

FIRST IMPRESSIONS LAST

Steve Thompson also made an immediate impact for City. A signing from Luton Town, he came on at the half-time interval of the clash at Oxford United in October, 1990. After a classy first contribution set City on the attack, Thompson went on to add City's second goal in a 2-1 win with a sparkling finish. He side-stepped a challenge on the edge of the penalty area and sent a curling right-foot shot beyond the goalkeeper's fingertips and into the corner of the net. Thompson went on to make more than 150 appearances for City before leaving for Burnley.

TOP TUNES

For some people, the top songs of 1974 included Kung Fu Fighting, Seasons In The Sun, Waterloo and You Ain't Seen Nothin' Yet. What do they know? In Leicester, the nightclubs throbbed and the young people danced away their cares to the classic This Is The Season For Us, sung by Leicester City's players. It is the number one track on the Filbert Street

Blues CD, released by those good folk at Cherry Red Records, that brings together all your favourite City songs on one disc. That's right, all of them. All 19 of them are there for your listening pleasure.

This Is The Season For Us is the best of a bad bunch – not that that's saying much – and the chorus goes like this:

> We've got the best crowd in England
> They're going to back us all the way, yes!
> This is the season for Leicester City
> It's Leicester, Leicester all the way

Two decades later, an ever-so-slightly funkier version of the tune was released and there are plenty of other priceless gems on the CD. The FNF rap appeared at the height of Family Night Football's popularity when the club encouraged young families to attend reserve-team matches. The rap included the lines:

> Filbert Fox the rapper
> Looking rather dapper
> City's leading clapper

All spat out by someone who wants to sound like Vanilla Ice, who had a number one hit in the 1980s and then almost got punched by former Leicester striker Stan Collymore when they were chucked together in the *Celebrity Big Brother* house on Channel Four's reality television show. Elsewhere on the CD, there's a song Oh Leicester City (calypso) by a group called The Back Five that is truly appalling, while Kev Price and the City Strikers aim straight for the heart with their non-hit Flowing Tears (Wembley 1993). If you think losing the play-off final against Swindon Town made you feel bad, wait until you hear that. The final track on the CD is We're Back Where We Belong, a tune that definitely belongs in the bargain bin.

DARK DAYS & DAVIES

The Jimmy Bloomfield era was followed by the Frank McLintock error. As a player, McLintock made 200 appearances for Leicester, appeared in the

FA Cup Finals in 1961 and 1963 and then left for Arsenal for an £80,000 fee that was a record sum paid for a City player. It proved to be money well spent. McLintock was named Footballer of the Year in 1971 after helping the Gunners to the league and FA Cup double and he was awarded a CBE. So, he was regarded as something of a returning hero when appointed Leicester manager in the summer of 1977. Not for long he wasn't.

His reaction to an early-season slump was to sell Frank Worthington and City fans watched their former idol go on to top the Division One scoring charts with Bolton Wanderers. As City headed for the drop, McLintock considered re-registering himself as a player and then wasted a club record £250,000 on former Derby County striker Roger Davies before deciding to walk the plank in April, 1978. City were relegated after netting just 26 goals – a record low for a 42-league game season until Stoke City scored 24 in 1984-85.

MATT FINISH

Matt Gillies was a rather more successful player turned manager. He made 103 appearances and scored eight goals before masterminding one of City's most successful spells in their history. In his decade in charge, City reached two FA Cup Finals, lifted the League Cup and had an unbroken spell in the top division.

NOT KELLY'S HEROES

Robert Kelly made 27 appearances for City – netting one memorable goal against Manchester United – and went on to manage the club in January, 2006. He had been assistant to Craig Levein and following his departure, Kelly steered City to Championship safety. But the Foxes were in relegation trouble again in April, 2007 when Kelly was sacked.

DOWN

Arthur Lochhead is another former player who took on the manager's job. Nine years after his playing debut, he became boss, but couldn't keep City in the First Division. Leicester finished seventh the following season and a boardroom bust-up led to Lochhead's departure early in 1936-37.

WHO NEEDS MONEY?

All the talk before the 1997 Coca Cola Cup Final at Wembley was about Middlesbrough's big-money foreign imports Juninho, Ravenelli and Emerson. Hardly a column inch was devoted to Leicester City and they were deserving of plenty. Martin O'Neill had worked wonders in taking City to their first major domestic final since the 1969 FA Cup Final defeat against Manchester City – and he masterminded the revival in quick time.

Twelve months to the day before City took on Middlesbrough, Leicester were seventh in the second tier of English football after a win at Crystal Palace and clinging to the hope that a late run of good form could power them into the play-offs. They did just that and victory over Crystal Palace in the play-off final propelled the Foxes into the First Division. City were tipped for relegation and along with defying the bookies, they also claimed wins over Scarborough, York City, Manchester United, Ipswich Town and Wimbledon to get through to the Coca-Cola Cup Final against Middlesbrough and secure the chance to clinch their first piece of silverware since they lifted the League Cup in 1964. The form guide suggested the cup was heading to Teesside. Three weeks before the clash at Wembley, Middlesbrough's Brazilian schemer Juninho had inspired his side to a 3-1 win in the Premier League at Filbert Street. O'Neill, of course, was determined that there would be no repeat in the cup final – even if it meant Pontus Kaamark faced a moral dilemma.

Kaamark was handed the job of man marking Juninho. A stylish player with caps for Sweden, Pontus admitted afterwards that he didn't feel that comfortable in the role of enforcer, but it didn't stop him doing a good job. Within a few minutes of the opening whistle, Juninho had felt Kaamark's boot and the shackles remained fastened until the final whistle. The sun shone on the 76,757 crowd and they saw City striker Emile Heskey and Fabrizio Ravanelli both hit the woodwork. The scoreline remained blank after 90 minutes and the deadlock was finally broken in the 95th minute when Boro's former Derby County striker Ravanelli smacked his shot past City goalkeeper Kasey Keller to put the favourites on course to lift their first major trophy.

City had other ideas, of course. They piled on the pressure and with just three minutes left in extra time, there was a massive scramble in the Boro penalty area and Heskey was on hand to force the ball home to earn a replay…

BORO BASHERS

So we all headed off to Hillsborough 10 days later for the replay… In their two Premier League games played since the draw at Wembley, City had fought out a 1-1 draw at Everton and lost 2-0 at Arsenal and that form wasn't enough to make anyone change their minds about who was going to win the Coca-Cola Cup when Leicester and Middlesbrough clashed again. As with the first meeting, Boro were the favourites and darlings of the national media and as before, there wasn't much between the sides in front of a crowd of 39,428. A City defence superbly marshalled by skipper Steve Walsh denied Middlesbrough many sights of goal and Leicester didn't give Boro keeper Ben Roberts many anxious moments in a goalless 90 minutes.

The final went into extra time and City made the breakthrough with 100 minutes on the clock. Garry Parker's free kick from the left picked out Walsh at the far post and he sent his header back across goal. Steve Claridge, his socks down by his ankles as always, squeezed between two 'Boro defenders and got on top of the ball to steer his right-foot shot beyond Roberts' fingertips and into the corner of the net. Middlesbrough's fans behind the goal sat in stunned silence while the blue half of Hillsborough erupted and within 60 seconds of Claridge finding the target came the moment that broke Boro hearts. Emerson was sent racing clear with just Kasey Keller to beat and City's goalkeeper raced from his line to block the Brazilian's shot. Leicester fans chanted: "USA" at ear-splitting volume in tribute and Keller admitted afterwards that he almost shed a tear when he heard that. After that, Boro's expensively assembled, cosmopolitan strikeforce seldom looked likely to grab an equaliser as Walsh marshalled Leicester's defence superbly.

Claridge, the hero in the dramatic play-off final win over Crystal Palace 11 months earlier, was substituted to a standing ovation and the final whistle was blown three minutes later. Walsh was named Man of the

Match and became the first City skipper for 33 years to get his hands on a major knockout trophy when he lifted the Coca-Cola Cup aloft to the acclaim of the wildly rejoicing Leicester fans. The victory also secured Leicester's first venture into European competition for more than three decades and completed an astonishing turnaround for the club under the leadership of manager Martin O'Neill. Ironically, Boro's line-up in both finals included future City boss Nigel Pearson.

TO THE RESCUE

The combined talents of Frank Worthington, Keith Weller and Steve Whitworth couldn't keep Leicester City out of the drop zone going into the closing weeks of the 1974-75 season. Foxes boss Jimmy Bloomfield issued an SOS to Chris Garland and in the space of just ten games, the flame-haired hitman became a Leicester legend.

In March, Bloomfield went back to former club Chelsea to sign Garland for £95,000 and he repaid the investment with eight goals to help keep City in the top flight. After making his debut in a 2-2 draw at Coventry City, Garland helped Leicester take a point from a clash with Liverpool at Filbert Street and remembered: "That result gave players like Weller and Worthington the confidence to play at their best." Three days later, Garland was the hat-trick hero in the 3-2 win over Wolverhampton Wanderers that took the Foxes out of the bottom three. Garland went on to find the target five times in just three games to fire the Foxes to the brink of top-flight survival.

Garland then grabbed five goals in just three games to help Leicester take a huge stride towards securing safety. He was on target in a 2-2 draw at Leeds United and then bagged two goals in both the 3-0 win over West Ham United on April 1st and the 4-0 demolition of Newcastle United that followed four days later to lift City up to 17th in the table. They were 15th after Worthington's goal secured a 1-0 win over Middlesbrough at Filbert Street which was enough to keep City in the top division.

Leicester survived despite taking only one point from the final three games of the season and went into the 1975-76 campaign with realistic hopes of qualifying for Europe. They missed out after finishing seventh – despite ending the season with a 2-1 win over Manchester United secured by Garland's winner – and after 63 games and 19 goals for Leicester, he went on to rejoin boyhood heroes Bristol City for a fee of £110,000 in November, 1976 and lead another successful survival fight. Garland was on target four times in three games to help keep the Robins in the First Division and he shrugged off several injuries to continue playing until he had taken his career tally of goals in all competitions to 103 in the 1982-83 season.

Garland was revealed to be suffering with Parkinson's disease in 1992 and in 2006, he underwent major brain surgery to help treat the condition. He has chronicled the events of his colourful football career and struggles after that in his book *A Life Of Two Halves*.

FRIENDLIES

Most of the 32,086 fans at the Walkers Stadium on August 8th, 2003 were there to see one man. Three weeks after Ronaldinho joined Barcelona in a £21 million transfer from Paris St. Germain, the Brazilian was lining up against Leicester City in a pre-season friendly. City boss Micky Adams was preparing his side for the start of the Premier League following the previous season's promotion and ten of his summer signings made an appearance – including former England international Les Ferdinand. But the game was really about Ronaldinho, a World Cup winner the previous summer and regarded as one of the best players on the planet.

He had snubbed a possible move to Manchester United to join the Spanish giants and had a starring role in Barca's 1-0 win at Leicester that was watched by Gary Lineker, who played for both clubs. City made them battle hard for victory. After Leicester goalkeeper Ian Walker denied Ronaldinho an early opener, Barcelona were reduced to ten men. Phillip Cocu was given his marching orders in the 20th minute for hacking down Craig Hignett, but Barcelona led at the break through Javier Saviola's sweetly-struck goal following good work from Ronaldinho. He was given a standing ovation when he was substituted after 61 minutes.

TOP SCOTS

City celebrated their centenary with a friendly against Aberdeen at Filbert Street in August, 1984. Alex Ferguson had made Aberdeen the leading force in Scottish football – leading them to the European Cup Winners' Cup in 1982-83 – and they held Leicester to a 1-1 draw. Steve Lynex got City's goal from the penalty spot.

NOT ALWAYS

Friendlies aren't always very friendly. Five days before the centenary match against Aberdeen, Ian Wilson was sent off in City's 2-2 draw against Rangers at Ibrox.

AGAINST GERMAN FRIENDS?

David Lowe suffered a shattered cheekbone in another less than friendly pre-season warm up. He made a £200,000 move from Ipswich Town in the summer of 1992 and the striker was then ruled out of the start of the following season after being injured in the clash against German side Borussia Monchengladbach at Filbert Street. Brian Little's side were beaten 3-1.

FOREIGN LEGION

Leicester City boss Tom Mather thought Frank Soo was a Foxes player – and got a shock when he looked at Port Vale's team sheet! Soo, the first player of Chinese extraction to play in the Football League, was a high-profile signing for City when he joined in September, 1945 after 12 years at Stoke City alongside Stanley Matthews. A regular for England in Wartime and Victory fixtures, he cost City a fee of £4,600 at the start of the first post-war campaign – and his midfield skills soon made an impression before the event that led to his departure from Filbert Street. Soo played as a guest for Port Vale in a fixture on Christmas Eve, 1945 without gaining City's permission and was immediately placed on the transfer list by Foxes boss Mather. The dispute led to Soo leaving City for Luton Town at the end of the season for £3,000 after just 16 appearances for Leicester and three goals.

NICE ONE THEO

Greece stunned world football when they won the European championships in 2004 – and holding aloft the trophy at the end of it all was a former City player. Theo Zagorakis led his country to victory in Portugal four years after leaving City. He came to Filbert Street in February, 1998 for a fee of £250,000 with an impressive CV having been named Greece's Player of the Year in 1997 and helped PAOK dump Arsenal out of the UEFA Cup. Zagorakis, a stylish midfielder, made his debut as a substitute against Leeds United in February, 1998 and went on to make 68 appearances for the Foxes before returning to Greece with AEK in the summer of 2000.

PONTUS MADE HIS MARK

Pontus Kaamark had already made his mark in world football before he joined City from Swedish club IFK Gothenburg for £840,000 in September, 1995. He was a regular in the Swedish national team and had been a part of the squad that finished third in the 1994 World Cup. Kaamark didn't have the best of luck with injuries early in his Leicester career and put that behind him to become a crowd favourite. He played a key role in City's Coca-Cola Cup triumph in 1997 with his shackling of Middlesbrough's Brazilian playmaker Juninho.

MISSED THE BUS

Leicester Fosse took to the pitch for the start of the 1892- 93 season without their goalkeeper! After Jimmy Thraves missed the bus to the season's opener at Mansfield Town; three goals flew past stand-in Kiddy Lowe before he got there. After Thraves arrived, Lowe went on to score Fosse's goal in a 4-1 defeat. Thraves made it in time for the start of the next match at Rotherham and was kept busy as Fosse were hammered 6-1.

LATE

In December, 1907, Fosse striker Fred Shinton turned up half an hour late for the game at Barnsley after his train was delayed. Fosse were still 3-1 winners in the Division Two clash.

TEAM ON THE RUN!

There was a mix up before Leicester City's clash at Crystal Palace in September, 1922. A London charabanc driver delivered the team to the Crystal Palace believing the team were competitors in a band festival! He managed to get them to Selhurst Park just in time for kick-off and all the upheaval didn't bother the team. They were 1-0 winners through a goal from Dennis Jones.

OH, SWEET LORD

At least the above all made it to the game. George Harrison missed his farewell match for Leicester Fosse! He missed the train to what was set to be his last game in Fosse colours at Bradford Park Avenue on October 16th, 1915. A friend of a Fosse player, named Cope, ended up playing after going along to watch and Leicester won 2-1.

THAT'S NOT THE TICKET

Billy Dorrell suffered a similar fate. He made a popular return to Leicester Fosse from Aston Villa in the 1895-96 season and marked his first appearance back with a goal in the 5-0 thumping of Burslem Port Vale. He then helped Fosse to a 2-0 win at Burton Swifts before missing his train for the home date with Rotherham Town. He must have had mixed emotions when he learned Fosse had won 8-0 without him, but he was back in the side for the next match.

WHO'S THE DADDY?

Matt Elliott had other things on his mind, but it didn't show. Elliott's wife took her place among the crowd at Wembley for the Worthington Cup Final between Leicester City and Tranmere Rovers on February 27th, 2000 despite expecting to give birth to the couple's fourth child that very day! He put that behind him to power City to victory in a historic match.

Leicester's 2-1 win meant they lifted the first major trophy of the new millennium and also won the last League Cup Final to be held at the old

Wembley. City had become quite used to playing at the old place – this was their seventh trip to the Twin Towers in nine years – and Elliott was the two-goal hero against a Tranmere side led by former Foxes striker David Kelly and containing the throw-in launcher David Challinor.

However, it was City who took the lead from a set piece. In the 29th minute, Guppy swung over a corner that Elliott headed home while Muzzy Izzet missed the chance to double the lead when he shot wide from a good position on the hour. Tranmere were dealt a massive blow three minutes later when defender Clint Hill was red carded after clattering into City striker Emile Heskey on the edge of the penalty area. As often happens, the dismissal fired up the side reduced in numbers and Rovers were level in the 77th minute. Kelly latched on to a flick on and steered his shot into the City net. But the sides were on level terms for just three minutes.

Elliott was on target for City again with another header from a Guppy corner and, unsurprisingly, his two goals earned him the man-of-the-match award at the final whistle. He had more to celebrate a few days later when his wife gave birth. Elliott had also been on target in the semi-final victory over Aston Villa. He had been pushed into the forward line after Martin O'Neill's side were hit by injuries and came up with the only goal of the two-legged affair with City's Midlands rivals. The first leg at Villa Park ended goalless and that prompted the home side's manager John Gregory to make some ungracious comments about Leicester not crossing the halfway line. He was gleefully reminded of those remarks by City fans after Elliott's header in the second leg at Filbert Street hit the back of the net to send Leicester back to Wembley for a third League Cup Final in four years.

HANGING AROUND

Sep Smith is in Leicester City's record books for having the longest first-team career with the club. He made his debut on August 31st, 1929 and his last game came 19 years and 249 days later on April 14th, 1949.

In between those dates, Smith made an astonishing 586 appearances – ranking him second in the club's list of highest appearance makers behind Graham Cross on 599 – and ensured that City fans of a certain vintage got all misty eyed when he walked onto the Filbert Street pitch after the final game there against Tottenham Hotspur in May, 2002.

Smith was the seventh of seven brothers from Whitburn, County Durham – Tom also played for City – and the 1934 FA Cup semi-final against Portsmouth at St. Andrew's brought him face to face with brothers Willie and Jack. Pompey clinched a trip to Wembley with a 4-1 victory. Sep had been spotted by City's scouts while playing in a North versus South schoolboy trial match at Filbert Street in March, 1926 and Foxes boss Willie Orr soon moved to sign the promising teenager.

He made his debut rather prematurely as a 17-year-old with the local press reporting that he was "unable to pull his weight" when he took his place in the forward line in the absence of the ill Arthur Lochhead in the 3-2 defeat at Huddersfield Town on the opening day of the 1929-30 season. Smith, top scorer for the reserves in 1930-31 with 19 goals, went on to blossom in a deeper, right-half role in the 1930s that was better suited to his distributive skills and it was a surprise that he was rewarded with only one cap for England – as a second-half substitute against Scotland in the Jubilee international in 1935. He won the Second Division with City in 1937 and there were those who hoped he would be called up to replace the injured Don Revie for the Foxes' first appearance in the FA Cup Final in 1949.

Instead, he missed out in the reshuffle and made his final appearance for City seven days later in the 1-1 draw at Cardiff City that ensured Leicester maintained their record of never having played outside the top two divisions in English football. Smith was still at Filbert Street at the start of the following season as coach and a testimonial fund raised him £2,100. The departure of boss Johnny Duncan and arrival of Norman Bullock in December, 1949 led to Smith's departure from the club.

MILAN IS A LEICESTER FAN

Milan Mandaric completed his takeover of Leicester City in February, 2007 – and the club's fans celebrated. Mandaric had turned Portsmouth from second-tier strugglers into a Premier League force and planned a similar revolution at the Walkers Stadium. But he had to find the right man to take City to the top – and that wasn't going to be easy.

Two months after Mandaric took charge, manager Robert Kelly was on his way out of the Walkers Stadium. Kelly was sacked after a 3-0 defeat at Plymouth Argyle left City hovering just above the Championship drop zone with five games left and Mandaric turned to former Norwich City boss Nigel Worthington to keep the Foxes up. He did just that thanks to back-to-back wins at Preston North End and Barnsley – and then left the club at the end of the season!

Mandaric's search for a new manager took him to MK Dons and Martin Allen. He was appointed in May, 2008 and lasted just three months. During that time, he made an astonishing 16 signings, but it was his insistence that City shouldn't sign Jimmy Floyd Hasselbaink that apparently led to him leaving after just four Championship games in charge. Mandaric was reportedly keen for City to sign the former Chelsea marksman, Allen wasn't. Ironically, Allen's last game in charge brought City's best performance in a season that ended in relegation to the third tier of English football. His team handed out a 4-1 thrashing to Watford at the Walkers Stadium and four days later, Allen left the club by mutual consent. Gary Megson then became City's fourth manager in Mandaric's seven months at the helm when he took on the job in September, 2007. Megson had been out of management since leaving City's East Midlands rivals Nottingham Forest 19 months earlier – and stayed at Leicester for just 41 days!

He took charge of nine games in the Championship and then left to take on the manager's job at Premier League side Bolton Wanderers, much to the dismay of Mandaric and City's supporters.

Mandaric went on to appoint Ian Holloway as manager. He made the move from Plymouth Argyle and ended up going into City's history books for all the wrong reasons. Holloway was at the helm when the Foxes suffered the drop into the third tier of English football for the first time in their history following a goalless draw at Stoke City in May, 2008.

Holloway was sacked and Nigel Pearson took on the manager's job...